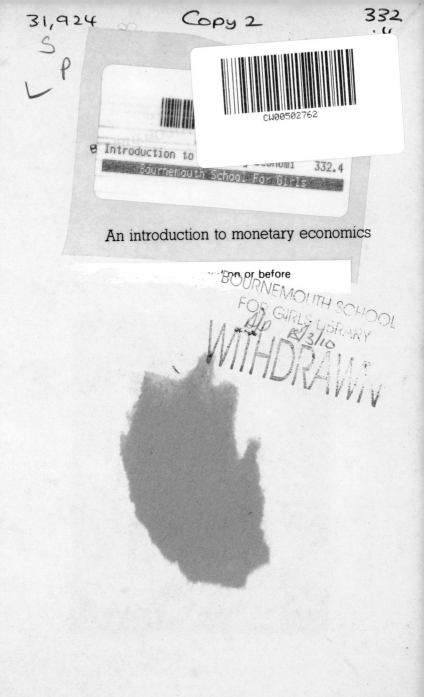

P.G.A. Howells and K. Bain

AN INTRODUCTION TO

MONETARY
ECONOMICS

LONGMAN
London and New York

Longman Group Limited
Longman House, Burnt Hill, Harlow
Essex CM20 2JE, England
Associated companies throughout the world

Published in the United States of America
by Longman Inc., New York

First published 1985

British Library Cataloguing in Publication Data

Howells, P.G.A.
   An introduction to monetary economics.
   1. Money
   I. Title   II. Bain, K.
   332.4   GH221

ISBN 0-582-29663-3

Library of Congress Cataloging in Publication Data

Howells, P. G. A., 1947–
   An introduction to monetary economics.

   Bibliography: p.
   Inlcudes index.
   1. Money.   I. Bain, K., 1942–
II. Title.
HG221.H8525   1985   332.4   84–14346
ISBN 0–582–29663–3

Set in 10/11pt Linotron 202 Rockwell
Printed in Singapore by
The Print House (Pte) Ltd

Contents

Money is controversial. How to control the supply of it, what it does, and even what it is are matters of argument and often quite bitter dispute.

Money is also mysterious. People find it difficult to understand how something seemingly as tangible as money can be increased or decreased by strokes of a pen or presses on a computer keyboard. The ease with which banks can so act and the very small costs involved deepen the mystery.

There is mystery, too, in the language of money – a language which (like most technical language) might have been designed to aid precision and to reduce confusion among those who use it. It might have been; but there is room for a sneaking suspicion that a language that needs to refer to the man in the street as part of the 'non-bank private sector' and to cheques as 'negotiable instruments' is intended to close the doors of a prestigious club firmly in the face of non-members. Whether that be so or not, the language of money is discouraging to the beginning student. Money may talk, but what is said about it needs translation.

Finally, money can be confusing. There lingers in the minds of most newcomers to the subject a feeling that some physical commodity **must** ultimately be supporting the vast pyramid of cheque accounts; that somehow the writing of a cheque is just a convenient substitute for 'real' payment (in notes and coin, or even gold) which could ultimately be demanded.

No book, certainly not a brief introductory one, could claim to unravel all the mystery, much less resolve the controversy. As in so many activities, confidence in monetary economics comes with understanding and that, in turn, comes with practice and familiarity. We can, however, hope to reduce the confusion and to encourage rather than deter those who are making a start.

PREFACE

The book is directed towards those studying economics at 'A' level, at first-year undergraduate level and at the intermediate level required by professional examinations such as those of the Institute of Bankers. It assumes, for the most part, that readers have a prior acquaintance with the principal relationships of macroeconomics but is meant to be accessible also to those studying concurrently such relationships for the first time.

P.G.A.H.
K.B.

Acknowledgements

The thoughts we have here committed to paper are the outcome of many influences. Among the most valuable have been the discussions with colleagues, with our undergraduates and with visitors to the North East London Polytechnic conferences for students and teachers of 'A' level economics. We acknowledge this with pleasure and with thanks.

In the latter stages of preparing the text we have received particularly helpful comments from Brian Henry, Keith Cuthbertson, Richard Powell and Peter Mottershead. For their generosity we are especially grateful. Like all authors, however, we claim complete originality for the errors.

Our thanks also go to Pat Norris for her help with typing the manuscript.

We are grateful to the following for permission to reproduce copyright material:

Bank of England for extracts from p 8 *Competition and Credit Control* (1971), p 197 *Bank of England Quarterly Bulletin* (June 1983), table 3.2 from table 3.1 *Bank of England Quarterly Bulletin* (Dec 1983), table 3.1 from p 79 *Bank of England Quarterly Bulletin* (March 1984); Financial Times for table 4.3 *Financial Times* (24/9/83); Heinemann Educational Books Ltd for part table 4.4 from p 106 *The Framework of United Kingdom Monetary Policy* (1982) ed. David Llewellyn; The Controller of Her Majesty's Stationery Office for an extract from p 1 *The Government's Expenditure Plans 1980–81* (Cmnd. 7746), and part tables 4.4, 6.3, 6.4 from tables in various issues *Economic Trends* and *Financial Statistics*; Institute of Bankers for three questions *Monetary Economics Paper* (April & Sep 1982); Institute of Cost and Management Accountants for a

ACKNOWLEDGEMENTS

question from *Economics Paper* (1981); Joint Matriculation Board for examination questions *Economics Advanced Paper* (June 1974, 1977, 1980, 1982) and *Economics Special Paper* (June 1975, 1977); University of Cambridge Local Examinations Syndicate for an examination question *Economics & Public Affairs* Paper 1 (1982); University of London University Entrance and School Examinations Council for examination questions *Economics Paper 1* (code 120) A Level (Jan 1981, Jan 1982, June 1982, June 1983) and *Economics Special Paper* A Level (June 1978); Oxford Delegacy of Local Examinations for examination questions *Economics Paper S* A Level A–40–S (June 1980) and *Economics Paper 1* A Level A–40–1 (June 1979 and July 1981); Welsh Joint Education Comrhittee for examination questions A Level *Economics A2 Part II* (June 1978 & June 1980).

Abbreviations

Throughout the text the following abbreviations have been used to identify the examination bodies who have been kind enough to let us use their past examination questions:

C   University of Cambridge Local Examinations Syndicate
I of B   Institute of Bankers
JMB   The Joint Matriculation Board
L   University Entrance and Schools Examination Council of the University of London
O   Oxford Delegacy of Local Examinations
WJEC Welsh Joint Examination Committee
ICMA Institute of Cost and Management Accountants

1 INTRODUCTION

1.1 MONEY AND OTHER VARIABLES

Our interest in money, as students of macroeconomics, stems principally from three important links: with expenditure; with output and employment; and with prices.

We are interested in expenditure decisions because these affect the community's welfare. In particular, more expenditure on new, domestically produced goods or on domestically provided services may lead to increases in output and employment. We are thus interested in the relationship between money and expenditure and, in turn, in the extent to which changes in expenditure influence the community's real income.

1.2 MONEY AND EXPENDITURE

At first sight it seems obvious that if there is more money there will be more spending. This is because our money balances seem to us, as individuals, the major constraint on our expenditure; and since our wants are limitless any addition to our money balances (as notes and coin in pocket or as a deposit in a bank account) is likely to be spent. Or, to look at things the other way round, the reason we would like more money is to enable us to buy more goods or services.

This apparently common-sense view is the basis of one of the oldest and best-known traditions in monetary thinking, i.e. that people hold money only in order to spend it. Money has no value in itself; it is worth only what it will buy. Anyone who receives income or has wealth which he or she does not wish to spend will

1

hold it in the form of assets other than money, i.e. assets which have some value in themselves in the sense that they will produce future income (as interest payments, dividends or capital gains).

The rational decision from this perspective is to hold only the minimum amount of money to avoid the inconvenience of barter until the next pay-day replenishes our pockets or bank accounts. On this view, an increase (for example) in the money stock, leaving people with excess money balances, will lead directly to an increase in expenditure on consumption or investment goods.

A little reflection, however, shows that the view that money is only wanted in order to spend (i.e. to undertake **transactions**), and that a change in the quantity of money available will change the level of expenditure, is too simple.

People do not as a rule hold the minimum balances necessary to see them through from one pay-day to the next. If we take Fig. 1.1 to illustrate the money receipts, money payments and money balances of a man paid £100 weekly, we can see that even though his total weekly payments are £100 and may **appear** to be regular and predictable he maintains some surplus – a precautionary balance, of, say, £10 – reflecting some uncertainty about the precise timing of receipts and payments. Assuming that he spends at a constant rate, his average money holdings measured over each week could be as low as £50 (the mid-point between £100 and £0) if he held the minimum balances necessary to finance transactions. But with a precautionary reserve of £10 the actual average balance is £60.

Once we acknowledge the holding of money balances in excess of the quantity strictly required for the purposes of transactions, it becomes at least theoretically possible for an increase or decrease in the money stock to find its way into larger or smaller precautionary balances. Whether a change in the money

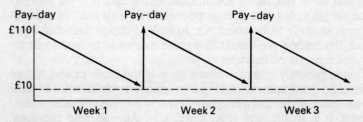

Fig. 1.1

supply does or does not find its way into these residual balances must depend on whether the motives for holding these balances are subject to change. It may be unlikely, but it is possible to imagine some increase in uncertainty about the future causing people to want to have more money at hand for use in emergency. We have, then, opened up the possibility that a change in the money stock does not have to lead to a change in expenditure. It may, rather, lead to a change in the amount of money which people hold in the form of precautionary balances.

Further, it is possible that a change in expenditure, consequent upon a change in the money stock, may not lead to the change in expenditure on goods which we have stressed is our principal concern. When people acquire extra money, the common-sense view tells us that they will seek to exchange it for other assets of various kinds. Some will then go to the purchase of real assets such as consumer durables and investment goods. But how does the purchase of financial assets affect prices and output?

The decision to buy more government stock or Ford Motor Co. shares does not of itself affect the price or output of government services or Ford cars. And yet it is perfectly possible for an increase in the money stock to be spent upon the purchase of such assets for at least two reasons. Firstly, such assets yield a money income in the form of interest or a dividend; secondly, their prices fluctuate and buying at the right time might produce for the buyer a subsequent capital gain. In the reverse way, a decrease in the money stock may be accommodated by a sale of such assets. Once again, a change in the money stock may not be immediately reflected in a change in expenditure on real goods.

However, we may regard this as an intermediate position since the purchase and sale of financial assets may not be the end of the process. The buying (or selling) of financial assets will affect the general level of interest rates and this may, in turn, influence some types of expenditure.

Consider the case of the government stock called 'Treasury 13 per cent 2000'. This is a promise to pay £13 per annum on every unit of stock held (actually in two six-monthly instalments of £6.50) and to pay to the holder of the unit £100 by way of 'redemption' in the year 2000. If the current holder of the stock paid £100 for its purchase he is receiving an annual payment which is effectively 13 per cent. Since such stock can be bought and sold, however, it is plainly possible that its price may fluctuate. In March 1984, for example, a buyer of our 'Treasury 13 per cent 2000' would have had to pay around £118 for it. Now, £13 paid on an outlay of £118 is less than 13 per cent; $13 \div 118 \times 100$ is equal to only 11 per cent.

If we generalise, now, from an individual government stock to financial assets as a whole, and from the individual purchaser to buyers as a whole, we can see that if an increase in people's money balances does find its way into financial assets, their price will rise and the effective rate of interest or yield will fall. This will make it cheaper for firms wishing to borrow by issuing new shares. Equally, if banks and other financial institutions are to retain their customers, they too will have to consider a reduction in the rates of interest charged. An increase in the money supply will cause downward pressure on interest rates; a reduction in the money stock will push them up. The implication for expenditure is that this will change if some expenditure decisions are sensitive to interest rates. In particular, expenditure upon 'real' assets which yield a future stream of earnings is likely to be affected. Any (given) expected level of future earnings from a machine or building, for example, now compares less favourably with the cost of borrowing to finance the project. If the intention was to plough back past profit, the same thing applies. The projected earnings from the real asset(s) are lower in comparison with the earnings from financial assets which might be purchased instead. In more formal terms, the net present value of all assets has fallen; we have moved up the 'marginal efficiency of capital' curve. By how much it will change will depend upon the pro-

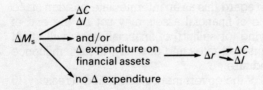

Key: C = consumption expenditure
I = investment expenditure
Δ = change in
M_s = money stock
r = interest rate

Fig. 1.2

portion of total expenditure which is affected by changes in interest rates and the sensitivity (or 'interest-elasticity') of that proportion. If we use conventional macroeconomic symbols we can summarise the possible money–expenditure links as in Fig. 1.2.

1.3 MONEY, OUTPUT AND EMPLOYMENT

Let us now concentrate on those cases where a change in the money supply does lead (along whichever channel) to a change in expenditure on goods and services. What is important is that such a change need not necessarily lead to a change in domestic output. One obvious possibility is that people or firms will change their expenditure on imported goods. This will not, of course, be the end of things. The change in expenditure on imports may affect the balance of payments and this, in turn, may lead (depending on the exchange-rate system in existence) to changes in the exchange rate. These changes may influence future expenditure decisions as well as influencing the attractiveness to foreigners of British exports. It is possible, then, that an increase in the domestic money supply will, in effect, flow out of the country, having no effect on domestic output.

Another possibility is that people will change their expenditure on domestically produced goods and services but shops will not (for some time at least) respond by changing their orders. They will just run down or build up stocks. Again, the expenditure – output link is broken.

Let us suppose they do change their orders and that output is changed accordingly. This does not necessarily lead to any immediate or even ultimate change in numbers of jobs. Firms, instead of creating new jobs, may increase levels of overtime worked or may attempt to increase the productivity of the existing workforce in a variety of ways. It is likely that falling orders will lead to fewer jobs, but this may take time. Changes in the number of jobs are always likely to lag behind changes in output.

We have, of course, one other important complication to consider: that is, a change in expenditure on domestic goods and services leads not to a change in output but to a change in the level of prices.

1.4 MONEY AND PRICES

Let us consider the way in which an increase in expenditure may present itself to a local shopkeeper. Our shopkeeper has been used to selling a known quantity of goods per period of time, at known prices, supported by a known quantity of stock which would meet customer's demands, with a small excess for unforeseen contingencies between the wholesalers' deliveries. There is now an increase in money balances which induces his customers to think of buying more. Suddenly, trade improves and the shopkeeper is faced with the prospect that his stock will run out and some customers will be disappointed.

If he has the facilities to handle the extra trade he could, however, phone the wholesaler and request emergency deliveries. These will be forthcoming if the wholesaler has the stocks, staff and transport to spare. By the same token, the wholesaler, finding the retailers that he supplies increasing their purchases from him, will seek to replenish his stocks from the manufacturers and the response that he gets will likewise depend upon their current operating position. If they have the capacity to do so, they will supply more.

The circumstances could, however, be quite different. The shopkeeper might already have all the trade he can handle without moving to larger premises and taking on more staff. The wholesaler may already be struggling to meet delivery dates with his existing vans and drivers. The producers may already be paying for overtime working. In this case the shopkeeper cannot meet the increased demand by increasing the quantity of goods for sale. Once he has sold his existing stock, customers will have to wait for the next deliveries. There is now a problem of allocation.

If he does nothing, the shopkeeper will be confronted on delivery day by crowds of customers all trying to be served before stocks run out. The goods may be rationed, perhaps on a first-come-first-served basis. The likelihood is, however, that the shopkeeper will see a short-run advantage at least in raising the prices he charges. Some customers may immediately go elsewhere but that does not matter since he would not have been able to supply everyone anyway. Initially he benefits by selling the existing quantity of goods at a higher price while his costs remain as they were.

We must remember, though, that this increase in demand resulted from an increase in money balances and will not apply to only one locality; it will be widely diffused. The story we have been telling will be repeated nationwide. Thus the wholesaler confronted by excess demand from his retailers will raise the price to all of them and the producer will raise the price to wholesalers when confronted by their demands for more. The rise in prices will be general and is likely to lead to demands for higher wages from workers. No greater quantity of goods will be bought, sold or produced. The increase in money balances is absorbed in conducting the same volume of trade at a higher price.

1.5 THE QUANTITY THEORY OF MONEY

This explains our statement that any increase in expenditure which cannot be met by an increase in output (or in imports) will result in a rise in prices, and the view that an increase in expenditure will lead to a change in price rather than quantity is, like the view that people want money only in order to spend it, a very long-established view in economics. It is part of what is usually referred to as the 'quantity theory of money'.

The most common expression of this is in the equation of exchange:

$$M_s V = PT$$

where M_s is the money stock, V the 'velocity of circulation' or the number of times the money stock changes hands per period of time, P is the average price of goods and services, and T is the number of transactions per period of time. It is customary to point out immediately that this is an identity or truism since $M_s \times V$ (the total of spending) must be equal to $P \times T$ (the total of receipts). In itself this is of no interest to us. What made the quantity theory a **theory** about behaviour and something worth believing in was that only two variables in the expression (M and P) were thought likely to change.

V was regarded as fixed by custom or convention. Note again the implicit view that money is used only as a medium of exchange. If, on the left-hand side of the equation, M_s increases, expenditure will rise because people's willingness to spend the money is fixed. On the right-hand side, T, the volume of transactions, will depend upon the **quantity** of goods and services bought and sold. This is taken to mean that it depends upon the quantity produced, though this assumes a constant relationship between total transactions and transactions involving newly produced goods and services. Thus, the transactions symbol (T) is often replaced by output (Y). This was traditionally treated as fixed because it was argued that the economy tended always to 'full employment' (though little thought was given to what was meant by the expression). The argument was that people would prefer to work rather than not work and that the force of competition for jobs would produce that level of real wage at which everyone could be profitably employed.

With V and T constant, a change in M_s will produce a proportional change in P.

It can be seen that we have combined the following two propositions:

(a) A change in the money stock will always produce a proportional change in expenditure, i.e. velocity is fixed.
(b) A change in expenditure will lead to a change in the price level rather than in the quantity of output.

This produces the basic monetarist conviction that a change in the money stock has its influence mainly upon the price level. Schematically, we have:

$$\Delta M_s \xrightarrow[\text{(a)}]{} \Delta \text{ expenditure} \xrightarrow[\text{(b)}]{} \Delta P$$

Link (a) arises because velocity is fixed; link (b) because output is fixed.

1.6 A SUMMARY OF ALTERNATIVE PROPOSITIONS

We can express in these same terms the propositions put forward earlier:

(c) A change in the money stock will simply lead to a change in the amount of money people hold in the form of idle balances, i.e. the velocity is variable and a change in M_s has no effect on the right-hand side of the equation of exchange. Schematically:

$$\Delta M_s \xrightarrow{} \Delta V$$

Students familiar with this area will recognise this as the case of the 'liquidity trap'. An intermediate case between (a) and (c) will, of course, have a change in M_s leading partly to a change in V and partly to a change in PT.

(d) A change in expenditure will lead to a change in output, i.e. output is not fixed at some constant level; T is variable. Again, we can have an extreme version with a change in M_s leading to a change only in T, i.e. prices remain constant; or we can have the intermediate proposition that the change in M_s affects both P and T.

Finally, we can also allow balance of payments involvement:

(e) A change in expenditure will lead to a change in the demand for imports and, hence, in the balance of payments and/or the exchange rate.

1.7 EXPENDITURE AND MONEY

This chapter has been written on the assumption that the change in money stock occurs first and causes changes in expenditure, prices and output. But if we acknowledge the possibility either that the government cannot control the money stock or that it is not willing to take the action necessary for it to do so, we must also consider the argument that the causal connection operates the other way round.

Suppose people's expenditure plans are determined entirely by factors other than their money holdings and that a change in one or more of these factors leads to a change in their desired expenditure. Suppose also that everyone is freely able to acquire the money which is needed to carry out expenditure plans. We then have:

$$\Delta \text{expenditure} \longrightarrow \Delta M_s$$

Alternatively, it is possible that if people cannot obtain the quantity of money they need, institutional changes will occur to enable the existing money stock to be used to undertake more expenditure, i.e. V increases. In this case, we have:

$$\Delta \text{expenditure} \longrightarrow \Delta V$$

9

In terms of the equation of exchange we may need to examine the proposition that:

$$\Delta PT \longrightarrow \Delta MV$$

1.8 THE NEED FOR A DEFINITION OF MONEY

We have been at pains in this opening chapter to establish a number of reasons for being 'concerned about' money in the economy. The first is that a change in the money stock could cause people to change their expenditure plans. Some economists rate the probability highly; others see a weaker link. Given that a change in monetary conditions at the very least **might** affect expenditure, there are further reasons for concern as changes in expenditure could affect prices or output and employment. Thus the concern is to understand the role that money plays in the economy.

One obvious prerequisite of any study of money is a definition of it. What exactly are we talking about? We could begin simply by saying that money is what most people (in our case, most economists) think it is. Unfortunately, even here economists cannot agree – providing good support for the popular view that any two economists hold between them three opinions. Even so, it would be simple if we needed only a broad, general idea of what money is.

Economists use the word 'money' in a broad way on many occasions. Thus, if you say 'this government is particularly concerned about the rate of growth of the money supply' or 'people wish to hold money balances in order to purchase goods and services', there is no difficulty in understanding you. But if you were to say 'Inflation is caused by too rapid a growth in the money stock', and someone else were to respond 'Money doesn't matter', how are we to prove who is right?

Again, if we wish to say anything more precise, – such as, for example, statements about **how much** expenditure will change in relation to a change in the money stock – we are going to have to deal with numbers. This will be the case above all if we wish, as many economists do, to use our understanding in order to intervene in the economy to push variables like unemployment and output to particular levels. Here the words 'by how much' will constantly recur.

Such quantitative information can be acquired by looking at the size of past changes in the money supply, output and employment and by carrying out tests of relationships between variables. Now, however, we shall need precise definitions. Without them, one might say, 'Let us test our statements using this definition of money'; and another might say, 'No, what I mean by money is . . .'.

Worse still, the way we define money is bound to be influenced by the view we have initially of the role of money in the economy. How we think money should be defined and how we think money interacts with other variables are ideas in joint supply. We might say that money is just another financial asset and so is quite similar to a number of other financial assets such as treasury bills, but is very different from bicycles. Or we might say that the way we look at things suggests that money is very different from everything else – as much different from treasury bills as it is from bicycles. Two economists may then be arguing about money but (as economists often do) they will not mean the same thing by the term.

If they each protect their own views by surrounding them with phrases such as 'in the long run' or 'in equilibrium' or 'other things being equal' or 'assuming no change in government policies' which are either vague or impossible to observe, they may be able to go on having their argument forever. In the meantime, governments act on the basis of one or other broad economic view and workers lose jobs, prices rise, exchange rates fall and some people become better off at the expense of others. It is thus important to know the terms of the argument.

Why is there any difficulty in answering the apparently simple questions: 'What is it that we are to count when we want to know the size of and changes in the money stock?' and 'Why can't we agree about the impact of such changes in the money stock on other economic variables?'

We may not, in the end, be able to resolve all these issues, but by the end of the book we shall at least be better able to understand *why* we cannot resolve them.

APPENDIX   Money links and textbook diagrams

In this appendix we want to relate the simple linkages outlined in Chapter 1 to some of the familiar textbook diagrams of

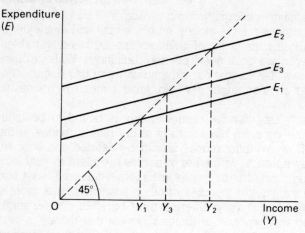

Fig. 1.3

macroeconomics. Consider, first, the possibility that an increase in the money stock, M_s, leads directly to an increase in either consumption or investment.

1. An increase in money supply and the 45° diagram

We begin in the normal way, assuming a closed economy with no government expenditure. The economy will be in equilibrium, with no tendency for the national income level to change, when expenditure equals income. The expenditure function (E) includes consumption and investment, with consumption assumed to be determined in the short run by income level while investment is assumed simply to be at some given level and **not** to be influenced by the level of income. In the jargon of economics, 'consumption' is said to be determined by income, *ceteris paribus*; 'investment' is said to be exogenously determined.

We shall, then, be in initial equilibrium in Fig. 1.3 at an income level of Y_1. If we make the beginning assumptions that we are talking here in terms of real income, that prices are constant and that the money stock does not change, clearly money does not enter the story at all at this stage. If, however, we allow Y to represent money income (able to increase therefore through either an increase in real income or an increase in prices), it is easy to consider the possibility that an increase in the money stock leads to an increase in total expenditure.

We can do this by assuming that prior to the increase in money stock, people and firms in the economy were happy to hold in the form of money balances the exact amount of the money supply, i.e. money supply was equal to money demand and the money market was therefore in equilibrium. The increase in the money stock now leaves people and firms temporarily holding higher money balances than they wish. At this stage, we discreetly do not ask how these additional balances have been acquired, although if we wish we can adopt Milton Friedman's example of money being dropped from a helicopter.

Obviously, people will take action to reduce their money balances to their previous levels – they will attempt to buy things. If they choose to buy real goods and services, money expenditure will rise. The expenditure line in Fig. 1.3 will move upwards from E_1 to E_2 and income will increase by a larger amount, rising from Y_1 to Y_2. The size of the increase in Y will depend upon the size of the multiplier, which, in turn, will depend upon the value of the marginal propensity to save (mps). The multiplier will be the inverse of the mps. We can refer to this rise in income as the **full** multiplier effect. Some of the increase in expenditure in this case will be in the form of consumption expenditure (video recorders, washing machines, etc.) and some will be in the form of investment (buildings, firm's plant and equipment, etc.)

Suppose, now, that people use their excess money balances **only** on purchasing additional financial assets. The prices of such assets will rise and interest rates will fall. If we further assume that consumption expenditure is unaffected by interest rate changes and that investment expenditure is not much affected by them, the total expenditure function will shift only to E_3 in our diagram.

The final possibility which we discussed in Chapter 1 was that people would choose to hold the increased money balances, rather than to spend them either on real goods and services or on financial assets. In this case, the expenditure function will stay at E_1 and income will not change.

In summary, it is possible for a change in the money supply to affect the level of expenditure significantly, slightly, or not at all. Of these three contrasting positions, we may say that the first resembles the monetarist view of the role of money in determining expenditure and the second, the Keynesian view.

2. Expenditure and price level changes

Our next concern was to distinguish between an impact on real income and an impact on prices. In the shopkeeper example we gave earlier, we dealt with two possible outcomes of the attempt of members of the public to spend their excess money holdings on goods and services: (a) that the goods would be supplied at no additional cost, and (b) that production and distribution conditions would mean that no more goods would be supplied. In the second case, the available supply would be rationed by price increases.

There is also the intermediate case where additional goods will be supplied but costs of production will be forced up and prices will rise. Costs will be expected to rise because we are dealing with short-run situations in which the capital stock of firms is assumed to be fixed. Consequently, as extra workers are hired in order to increase output their marginal product falls, average product falls, and average costs rise (the case of diminishing returns). These various possibilities can be seen on Fig. 1.4, which is an aggregate supply curve (AS) showing the receipts which firms require in total to induce them to supply any given volume of output. At first it rises at a constant rate because we assume

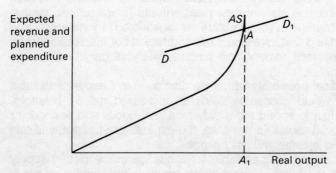

Expected revenue and planned expenditure

Real output

Fig. 1.4

14

that there is some considerable range of production over which unit costs are constant. Towards the right-hand end of the curve, however, firms require a progressively greater rise in revenue to induce any given increase in output. This becomes particularly marked as full employment is approached. Eventually, we reach the point A in Fig. 1.4 at which no further output is forthcoming whatever the expected revenue. Raising the aggregate demand curve above DD_1 produces no rise in real output, only a rise in price. It is along line AA_1 that the long-run equilibrium level of output is assumed to be by the quantity theory of money. We might also refer to this as the natural position of the economy. It is on this basis that we can assume T (transactions) to be constant in the equation $MV = PT$.

3. Full employment output

The argument that the economy will tend to settle at this level of output depends upon a particular, but very common, view of the operation of the economy's labour market, as shown in Fig. 1.5.

The essential element in this view is that wages are flexible downwards – that workers are willing and able to accept lower real wage levels in order to obtain jobs and that, therefore, as in other markets, supply will come to equal demand through changes in price, i.e. the wage rate. Thus, if we are temporarily at L_1 with a real wage of $\dot{W}_1$ and there are a number of workers

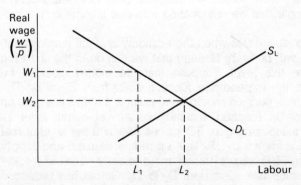

Fig. 1.5

out of work and genuinely seeking work, competition for the existing jobs will bid the real wage down to W_2. We shall reach an equilibrium and we can take L_2 as being the point of full employment, defining full employment as a state where everyone who is able and willing to work **at the existing wage rate** has a job. There may still be workers who see themselves as unemployed and who are counted as unemployed in official statistics. These, however, can be considered as having been priced out of the labour market. They will only obtain work if the whole labour supply curve shifts down.

There are many difficulties associated with this story. Most obviously, workers do not directly determine the real wage for which they work. Workers apply for jobs at set rates of pay and trades unions bargain directly for money wage rates, not real wage rates. In more general terms, wages are not simply an economic variable and their level may be influenced by social institutional and historical factors as well as by demand and supply.

Whether or not the economy does tend naturally to a full employment position, it remains that if we happen to be at such a position then, irrespective of our definition of full employment, output will be prevented from responding to changes in expenditure and prices must bear the whole of the adjustment.

4. Inflationary gaps

Now we can return to the 45° diagram (Fig. 1.6) being careful this time to note that we are dealing with real income on the horizontal axis.

We can postulate that when the economy is at full employment, real income will be at Y_f. Nothing that we can do in the short run can increase this level. Suppose that the money stock is increased and the expenditure function shifts from E_1 to E_2. The new equilibrium position should be at point A, but this is a position which cannot be reached. Instead, we stay at output level Y_f. There is an inflationary gap, BC; prices rise until the level of **real** expenditure is shown by E_1. The aggregate demand and supply diagram (Fig. 1.7) shows things more clearly. The aggregate demand function has risen from D_1 to D_2. Output has remained constant but prices, and hence total revenue, have risen.

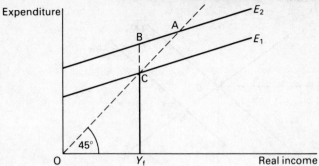

Fig. 1.6

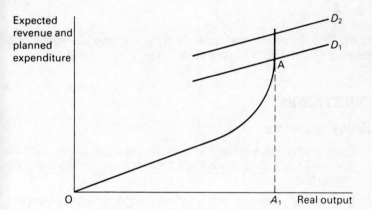

Fig. 1.7

5. The IS/LM story

Many students are familiar with IS and LM diagrams which show
the determination of equilibrium positions in the goods market
and money market, respectively. They may be used to tell an
alternative version of the same story as above. In Fig. 1.8 the
increase in money supply shifts the LM curve down to LM_2 as
people attempt to get rid of excess money balances. The new
equilibrium position should be at A, but this cannot be achieved.
Instead, prices are forced up and the real value of the money

17

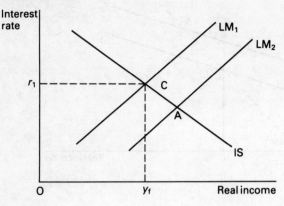

Fig. 1.8

stock falls. In effect, we move back to our original equilibrium point of C but with a higher price level.

QUESTIONS

Essay questions

1. Explain what is meant by the 'quantity theory of money'. Discuss how well this theory lends itself to an explanation of price inflation. (JMB).

2. How might a change in the money supply affect consumption and investment? (O)

3. Explain how a change in the money supply might influence investment (a) directly and (b) through changes in interest rates. In what circumstances might these links be weak?

4. Why is it important to know whether the velocity of circulation and/or output are constant in considering the relationship between the money supply and prices?

Discussion questions

1. Consider the relationship between interest rates and bond prices. Is the relationship affected by the date of maturity of bonds?

2. Investigate the relationship between interest rates and government bond prices in practice. Follow the price changes of particular government stocks over a period of some months.

3. Make sure that everyone in your group knows the distinction between cash and money. Why is it of benefit to individuals and to an economy as a whole to use money for exchange purposes rather than engaging in barter?

4. Why is it important to find a precise definition of 'money'? Why do you think there might be difficulties in so doing? Consider all the assets which you think do or could serve as money in an economy.

FURTHER READING

The quantity theory of money is set out in many texts. Vane and Thompson (1982) Ch. 3 has a brief account; as do Crockett (1979) Ch. 4 and most general macroeconomic texts. A much more useful treatment including material on the historical development of the theory is in Shaw (1977) Ch. 3. More advanced treatments include that by Pierce and Shaw (1974) Ch. 6.

The application of basic monetary theory in macroeconomic models and diagrams is dealt with simply in Dow and Earl (1982) Ch. 1 and much more thoroughly and formally in Laidler (1977) Ch. 1. The relationship between the prices of financial assets and interest rates is covered more formally than here in Rowan (1983) and in many other books.

2 MONEY IN THE ECONOMY

2.1 USES OF MONEY

It is common practice to list four or five roles of money. The problem is that these involve a variety of ways of looking at money and a variety of implications for measurement. It seems preferable to concentrate on the two uses of money which are important in economic theory. These are quite clear.

The first is that people, governments and firms use money to buy commodities. If we think of it only in these terms, money is anything which can be used to purchase goods and services. The word 'purchase' is important here and we shall need to consider later what we mean by it. Money held in order to enable goods and services to be purchased has been described as 'active' or as 'active balances'. This is simply a repetition of our central notion in Chapter 1 that people hold money in order to carry out transactions. All we have done is to turn it round to say: anything which people hold which enables them to carry out transactions is money.

The second reason for holding money is that it is one element in wealth. It is, as older books like to say, 'a store of value' – as, of course, are other forms of wealth such as buildings, stocks and shares, the plant and equipment of firms and inventories. The various forms of wealth have their own characteristics and there are reasons for wishing, in particular circumstances, to hold wealth in some forms rather than others. Money which is held because of its characteristics as an asset has been described as 'idle' or as 'idle balances'.

It is apparent that it is not possible to separate completely these two uses of money since some things (most obviously notes and coins) perform both functions. It is true that the two uses do not lead to coincident definitions of money. In addition, they lead to different answers to the important question of whether there are other assets which are good substitutes for money. Consequently, we shall look at each of them independently.

2.2 MONEY AND TRANSACTIONS

Let us return to our preliminary definition of money as 'anything which can be used to purchase goods and services'. We are ruling out the possibility of barter here because we are concerned with the acceptability of money in exchange for commodities generally.

By the phrase 'to purchase' we mean 'to obtain full legal ownership of'. Suppose a man buys a bicycle and pays for it in legally acceptable pound notes. He has at one moment entered into debt to the extent of the price of the bicycle and simultaneously settled that debt by handing over the pound notes. The bike is now legally his. There is no presumption on the part of the shopowner that he could have demanded payment in gold, nor that he could take the pound notes to a bank and insist on their conversion to gold (in spite of the legend printed on the face of UK bank notes). From this example, we can derive the notion of money as something which 'extinguishes debt'.

Suppose, however, a second man arranges to purchase a bicycle by entering into a hire purchase contract. He receives the bicycle and can use it but it is not yet legally his. If he does not keep up his payments (made in some form acceptable to the hire purchase company) the bicycle can be reclaimed. If he 'pays' for the bicycle with a credit card, Visa or Access may not have a specific legal claim on the bicycle, but they do have a general claim on the purchaser's property. He has only 'purchased' the commodity by entering into debt. It is clear that there is a considerable difference on this basis between pound notes and credit cards (or other ways of obtaining credit) and it seems reasonable to regard as money only those things which can be used to purchase goods and services, without entering into debt. Later, though, we shall need to make one important exception to this.

What, then, can we include? We can certainly include notes and coins (legal tender). (Remember, it is legal acceptability which is important, so counterfeit notes do not count.) A much

21

higher proportion of the total value of all transactions is, however, paid for by cheque drawn on sight deposits (sometimes known as demand deposits or cheque-account deposits) with clearing banks.

Suppose a woman pays for her bicycle with a cheque drawn on Lloyds Bank. Once the seller has deposited the cheque with a bank and the cheque has been cleared with Lloyds, the bicycle has been purchased. The seller's account with the Midland Bank has increased; the buyer's bank deposit with Lloyds has shrunk. The purchase has been made; notes or coins have not changed hands; no debt has been entered into. Money is obviously involved. But what is it that consitutes money? The important point is that Lloyds have been willing to clear the buyer's cheque, i.e. her sight deposit account has been sufficiently in credit to cover her cheque. She can go on writing cheques and buying commodities only for as long as this is true. There is no doubt here, then, that it is the sight deposit account that is money, not the cheque itself.

The existence of cheque-guarantee cards makes no difference to this. All they do, as in the case of credit cards, is to transfer the debt. Consider the case of someone who does not have enough in his sight account to cover a cheque which he writes. Assume, firstly, that this cheque is not backed by a bank cheque-card. The cheque bounces and the seller still legally owns the bicycle. If the cheque is backed by a cheque-card, the purchaser will have entered into debt with the bank. Now if the bank requires the immediate extinction of this debt, the existence of the cheque-card will have made no overall difference.

It remains true that it is only through having a sufficiently large amount in a sight deposit account that a person is able to purchase our bicycle without going into debt. It is also the case that it is only the bank clearing system which makes a sight deposit generally acceptable as a means of purchasing commodities, i.e. which enables someone, for example, to write a cheque on a Barclays account in Sunderland and use it to buy goods from a person with a National Westminster Bank account in Plymouth.

There are two apparent exceptions to the above statements that need to be dealt with; that is, there are two cases in which it may be possible to purchase goods without, at the time, having sufficient in a sight deposit account to cover the cheque. The first arises simply from the fact that cheques take a short time to be presented and cleared. A person may pay by cheque and depend upon his belief that by the time the cheque is presented for clearance his account will be sufficiently in funds. Here, though, it is still obvious that it is the contents of the account that constitute money. It is, therefore, no exception at all.

2.2.1 The importance of overdrafts

The second case is more important and gives rise to a point of overwhelming significance. This is where the bank manager agrees to allow a client to maintain an overdraft with the bank. This allows the client to write cheques to a greater amount than he has in his sight deposit account, in the knowledge that the bank will honour his cheques. Of course, in writing these cheques, the client is going into debt to the bank. The only difference between this and our cheque-guarantee card example is that the bank has agreed in advance to accept the debt. What makes it different from any other debt is that debt to a clearing bank **is** money since cheques incurring this debt are cleared by the bank.

This means that for as long as banks are prepared to give cheque books to members of the public with permission to write on the cheques and to circulate them, and for as long as they are prepared to carry out the clerical operation of moving figures from one column (customer A) to another column (customer B), banks have the power to create money. An obvious objection to this is that in the transfer from A's account to B's account 'money' which already existed has merely been redistributed. And so it has. But think of the overdraft case. Suppose A's account is empty but his bank grants him overdraft facilities. If A continues writing cheques to B, B's account gains until the overdraft facility is exhausted. A once again has a bank balance of zero but B has an increase in his money balances equal to the size of A's overdraft. Naturally, at some future date, A may be called upon to repay the overdraft and this he would have to do by draining other people's accounts into his. When he had done this, the overdraft would be paid off. His bank balance would still be zero but the money stock would have been reduced by the 'destruction' of the overdraft.

Jump, however, from the individual to the aggregate case and it is plain that increases by clearing banks in total overdrafts increase the money stock. The point cannot be overemphasised.

23

The size of the money stock is determined by what we shall call, for the moment, the banking system in the light of commercial prudence and the wishes of its customers. Money is not created and destroyed by the Central Bank or 'the monetary authorities'. They can only hope to influence the behaviour of those directly responsible – and experience suggests it is not easy (see Section 6.3).

2.2.2 Time deposits

There is one further complication which arises from these considerations. It is argued that other types of deposits with clearing banks should be included as part of the money stock. Time deposits are deposits which bear interest and for which notice of withdrawal is normally required. A bank may allow clients to overdraw sight deposit accounts, even if it has not agreed in advance to do so, if the amount overdrawn is covered by a time deposit. In this case, the time deposit becomes a substitute for a sight deposit and, it is claimed, should be counted as money.

There are several objections to this. Firstly, even though the bank will be charging a higher rate of interest on the overdraft than it is paying on the time deposit, it is unlikely to continue extending overdraft facilities on an ad hoc basis up to the full amount of the time deposit. Once one accepts that the time deposit is not, from the point of view we are here adopting, a perfect substitute for a sight deposit, it becomes difficult to say exactly how close a substitute it is.

Secondly, this argument only applies to cases where the time deposit and the sight deposit are with the same bank. The two are not substitutes for someone with a time deposit at the Royal Bank of Scotland in Glasgow and a sight deposit account with the Co-operative Bank in London.

Finally, when we are considering, later in the book, the factors that are likely to influence the amount of money people wish to hold, it will be useful to associate in our minds the reasons why people wish to hold money and the forms in which they will choose to hold it. It seems unlikely that anyone wishing to hold money to allow the purchase of commodities would choose to hold it in the form of a time deposit.

It seems far better, if we are concerned only with active balances, to limit our view of money to notes, coins and sight deposits with clearing banks, noting as we have done above that the total of sight deposits will be influenced by the amount which bank customers have overdrawn.

2.2.3 Building societies and luncheon vouchers

There remain a number of issues which frequently worry students and which need to be cleared up. The first concerns deposits with building societies. There is no doubt that, **from our present perspective**, building society deposits are **not** money. They cannot be used directly to buy goods and services or to settle past debts, because building societies do not engage in clearing operations. Thus, for most building societies, in order to use a deposit to purchase goods, a person needs to convert the deposit either into notes and coin or into a building society cheque written on a clearing bank. Both of these are money but both have already been included in our proposed measure of money above. Building society deposits can be converted into money but this does not, in itself, make them a substitute for money. Houses can also be converted into money but no one argues for their inclusion as part of the money stock. The question of the speed and safety with which other assets can be converted into money is not relevant here since our concern is simply with whether they can be used directly to purchase goods and services.

Confusion has arisen over the issuing of cheque books by some societies. We should observe, however, that in such schemes the building societies operate in partnership with banks which are part of the clearing system. If we look at what occurs when someone writes such a cheque to pay for goods, we will see that the argument in the previous paragraph continues to hold. A woman pays for her bicycle with a cheque drawn on her building society account. The seller presents the cheque to his bank which credits his account and clears the cheque with the bank associated with the building society. This bank, in turn, debits the account which the building society maintains with them and the building society debits the bicycle purchaser's account. All we have done is to add an extra stage. What makes the cheque acceptable is the deposit which the building society has with the banking system. It is this deposit which is money. The only change is that the building society has shown confidence in its clients by allowing them to write cheques in the building society's name without presenting themselves and their passbooks to the building society office. If people write cheques in excess of their building society deposits, they will have entered into debt with the building society. But this does not affect the size of the money stock from a transactions viewpoint since what we are counting as money is the building society deposit with the clearing bank. The only way the size of our money stock will be influenced is if building society clients write so many cheques that the building society account with the bank is overdrawn. This (unlikely) situation would be covered by our general treatment of overdrafts above.

Students are also sometimes confused over the existence of other limited ways of directly purchasing commodities. The most obvious example is that of luncheon vouchers. There is no doubt that they are a partial substitute for money, but the fact that they can be used to carry out only a limited range of transactions makes it sensible not to treat them as money. It is true, of course, that if people begin to receive luncheon vouchers, they may be able to buy the same value of goods as previously while needing to hold less money. Thus, the relationship between total expenditure and the money stock may change (i.e. the velocity of money may change).

There are many examples similar to luncheon vouchers – discount vouchers dropped through the letterbox which enable us to buy more margarine with the same amount of money as before; coupons obtained from cornflakes or soap-powder packets which enable us to have more train rides or cheaper groceries; cards which can be purchased and entitle us to discounts at certain stores; discount stamps which can be exchanged for goods: and so on. All of these reduce the amount of money that we shall need to hold in order to buy a given quantity of commodities; but all of them enable us to purchase only a very restricted range of goods, often within a limited time period and at a few places. It is an interesting exercise to see how many such devices one can think of.

Barter can achieve the same purpose as coupons and vouchers. Sometimes, it is possible to take books to a shop and exchange them for a smaller quantity of other books. However, the range and quantity of goods we can purchase with second-hand books is very small. This is not to say that barter is unimportant. (Indeed, it has been increasing in recent times, even at the level of international trade.) There are several football clubs, for example, which survive by exchanging young, promising players for a large number of older players. Again, though, the range of goods which can be purchased directly with a footballer is limited. Charlie Nicholas may be an asset to a football club, but a builder is unlikely to accept him as part payment for a grandstand.

The amount of bartering which goes on certainly influences the total value of transactions which can be undertaken with a given quantity of money, but goods which can be used in barter are not themselves money. It is best to regard luncheon vouchers and soap-powder packet coupons as modified barter rather than as money. Ultimately, when the vouchers, etc., are presented for payment to their issuers, they will be paid for by a cheque drawn on a sight deposit.

2.3 MEANINGS OF WEALTH

Let us now completely change our point of view and look at money as part of wealth. Before doing so, we need to spend some time discussing the idea of wealth.

We can begin by taking 'wealth' to mean the value of all assets held, whether by a person, a firm, the private sector of the economy as a whole, or a nation. In each case we could attempt to list all those things which might be regarded as assets and, hence, included in wealth.

2.3.1 Financial vs real assets

Such a list would be long and we would find it convenient to divide it into **financial assets** and **real** or **physical assets**. Financial assets are those which do not have an intrinsic value or use (they can not be sat upon or driven; they do not keep the rain out; they are not beautiful to look at, etc.) but they do have a value expressed in money terms. Financial assets include notes and coin, bank deposits, stocks and shares, life assurance policies, bonds, bills of exchange and many other similar assets.

The distinction between financial and real assets is particularly important in times of inflation. A financial asset, with a fixed monetary value, will lose value in real terms as prices of goods in the economy rise. The sale of a bond worth £100 will enable the seller to buy fewer and fewer goods as inflation proceeds. The prices of most real assets will, however, rise in line with the prices of goods and services and so the assets will retain their real value.

2.3.2. Individual vs aggregate wealth

This classification has other uses also but it does not get us far in the listing of assets. Imagine that we had to calculate the wealth of a rich businessman. What might we include? Houses, other buildings, rare paintings, jewellery, notes and coin, bank deposits, building society deposits, antique furniture, government bonds, motor cars, . . ., and so on.

Imagine next that we had to calculate the value of the wealth of the whole economy. Would we be able to include the assets of all individuals and firms? If we did, we would be engaging in a great deal of double counting since someone's financial asset is always someone else's liability. Your bank deposit is an asset to you but a liability of your bank, the businessman's shares in the British Oxygen Company are an asset to him but a liability of the company, and so forth. Apart from particular problems such as how to treat the liabilities of the government, we would find that financial assets cancelled out. We would be left with a long list of real assets, but the problems would just be beginning.

2.3.3. Valuing real assets

The major difficulty would be in putting a value on those real assets. Suppose we had to value our own individual real assets as a preliminary to estimating the value of all such assets in the economy. We could only place a value on items which had a value to other people. We could not include objects to which we were sentimentally attached but which meant nothing to anyone else. (Consider the difference between the gain to a burglar from his haul and the loss felt by the victim.) Consequently, one starting point would be to consider wealth as encompassing everything in existence at a point in time which has a market value, i.e. anything which can be exchanged directly or indirectly for something else. What problems occur if we take this approach?

. The principal ones relate to consumer-durable goods. Motor cars, TV sets, video recorders, home computers, refrigerators, etc., can all be regarded as assets. There are, however, clear difficulties in drawing a line between consumer-durable goods and non-durable goods. Many consumer durables depreciate rapidly in value. Does clothing in wardrobes count as wealth? Stocks of old records? Tinned food stored in preparation for the nuclear holocaust? Is there a dividing line? If so, where does it lie?

Further, although the second-hand sale value of consumer durables is often small (as is also sometimes the case with the plant and machinery of firms), their replacement value may be of more importance to their owners. Many people are willing to insure the contents of their homes at replacement cost, indicating that this might be the more correct valuation. This however, is obviously subjective. This approach does not seem to be getting us very far very fast.

2.3.4 Wealth as past savings

Let us try another angle. We could say that wealth consists of accumulated past savings and then ask what can legitimately be counted as savings rather than current consumption. One common response is to say that the purchase of consumer durables from which people hope to obtain future satisfaction represents saving. This introduces impossible questions as to how much saving should be attributed to each future time period. Individuals will apply different rates of depreciation to their purchases. For example, I may pay £60 for a bicycle and regard my saving this year as £60, next year as £45 and the following year as £30. I would be 'consuming' the bike at the rate of £15 per year. A more careful person who looks after his or her bike may estimate saving in each of the first three years of ownership as £60, £50 and £40, respectively.

2.3.5 Wealth and future incomes

It may seem that the question is easier if we think of wealth as capital and regard as wealth anything which can be used to produce a future income, either in the form of interest, dividend or rent payment or in the form of a capital gain. Then we can say that a washing machine in a laundromat is part of the economy's wealth, but a washing machine in the home is not; and that tables waiting in a warehouse to be sold are part of wealth, but tables in private homes are not. Or can we?

If we think in terms of decisions facing consumers, we still have to deal with a range of goods which can either be purchased outright or be rented. For these goods, it seems reasonable to adopt the usual opportunity cost approach and argue that such goods which have been purchased earn an implicit income equal to the rental which would have had to be paid to obtain an equivalent service. Since 'equivalence of service' is also subjective, we do not seem to have advanced at all. The idea is given credibility by people's willingness to borrow and to pay interest in order to buy consumer durables, but it leaves us without an adequate basis for attempting to measure the value of the stock of wealth.

2.3.6 Human capital

One way of attempting to introduce a degree of objectivity is to propose that wealth is anything which banks or other financial institutions are willing to allow to stand as security for a loan. This rules out a number of consumer durables which we might otherwise be tempted to include. However, this view raises an issue which was also implicit in our earlier approaches – the idea of human capital.

It is clear that one common use of past savings is to provide schooling or training and that this can be thought of as giving skills which may be sold in the labour market in return for a future income. Future incomes depend only to a relatively small extent on schooling, and a variety of other expenditures can be thought of as investments in the sense that they may increase future earnings. How, though, can one hope to provide a reasonable estimate of the total value of human wealth? The complications are numerous, as only one example: if we were to include the notion of opportunity cost, the ability of someone (not necessarily female) in a household to provide cooking and housekeeping services would have to be counted as part of the household's human wealth.

The best-known approach to attempting to measure total wealth, including human wealth, is Milton Friedman's notion of **permanent income**, where wealth is thought of in terms of people's anticipated future incomes and people are thought to base their expectations of future incomes on the incomes they have received over a number of past years. This excludes entirely the notion of opportunity cost and is limited in other ways. It has the advantage, however, of showing wealth (the present value of expected future income) and income to be two aspects of the one idea. It is a good example of a common phenomenon in economics – the need to find a measure which enables good predictions of future behaviour to be made. Such measures are often accepted despite their theoretical weaknesses.

2.3.7 Total private sector wealth

Another measure frequently adopted is that which includes only (a) government debt held by the private sector (notes and coin, government bills and bonds) and (b) the assets of the corporate sector, measured by the value of equities in companies. This is accepted as a measure of total private sector wealth simply on the grounds that it is possible to obtain figures for it. Everything else, including human capital, is omitted because other things are too difficult to measure.

2.4. MONEY AND OTHER FORMS OF WEALTH

The point of all this is that we must now consider why people or firms may choose to hold some of their wealth (however they value it) in the form of money rather than in other forms. There are two approaches to this question.

One is to think entirely in terms of the rates of return (including expected capital gains) which can be earned on different assets. All assets are regarded as having either an explicit or an implicit rate of return and everyone is assumed to be attempting to maximise the rate of return on his or her wealth, taking into account the different degrees of risk associated with various assets and the different attitudes towards risk which people have. Money is regarded as a special case since people wish to hold it for the purposes of transactions and because there is no explicit rate of return which reflects to people its usefulness as a medium of exchange. It is, then, very different from all other assets (see the earlier discussion in Section 2.2) and no other asset is a good substitute for it. On the other hand, there is no differentiation among all other assets. They are all (including Treasury bills and bicycles) equally poor substitutes for money.

The second approach is to concentrate on a characteristic of money other than its use in purchasing goods and services. This arises from the notion that all types of assets differ in the speed with which the value previously assumed by the owner can be realised in the market. That is, all assets can be sold fairly quickly, but many assets are such that a quick sale may only be possible at a much lower price than that at which the asset has been valued in a company's or a person's books or records. In other words, a quick sale may involve a considerable risk of loss; or to realise the asset's assumed value may take considerable time. Other assets are such that their value can be realised quickly with little risk of loss. This is the idea of liquidity.

Liquidity is a useful quality because it may enable wealth-holders to take advantage of opportunities in the market in order to make capital gains. For example, a person may anticipate that government bond prices will soon rise. If he can convert some of his wealth quickly and without loss into government bonds, he can hope to buy now and take advantage of the bond price rise when it comes.

Of more general significance is the fact that people or firms have liabilities which must be discharged at some time in the future. They need to keep their assets in a sufficiently liquid form to enable them to meet debts when they fall due for payment. Many firms have failed, not because of lack of assets but because the nature of their assets has been such that they have not been able to convert them into money sufficiently quickly for them to pay their bills on time. Everyone then has to attempt to match their assets to their liabilities in terms of degrees of liquidity.

In the light of this, we can see the special position of money to derive from the fact that (in money terms) money is the one asset which can never lose value which is always available to meet debts. It is the perfectly flexible or liquid asset which provides the standard by which the liquidity of all other assets can be judged. It also follows that, from the liquidity point of view, there are several assets which we earlier did not regard as money which might be thought of as money or near-money. Let us take some particular examples.

Almost certainly, from our present perspective, we should count time deposits with banks as money, since they can be converted into notes and coin, or sight deposits at very little notice and with, at most, the loss of only a small amount of interest. Many types of building society deposits are also either money or very-near-money. The only limitation on their liquidity up to quite large amounts is that offices of the societies are not always open. The existence of building society cheque accounts and of building society cash machines makes the deposits with societies even closer to money. Indeed, so close to money have they become that, as we shall see, the Bank of England now includes some building society deposits in one of its newer measures (M_2) aimed at providing an indication of the amount of money held for **transactions** purposes. Other short-term assets such as Treasury bills and government bonds near to maturity are very liquid. On the other hand, houses are, in general, illiquid assets and specialised capital equipment of firms may be highly illiquid.

Two points arise from this discussion. One is that it can be argued that there are many assets which are really rather good substitutes for money. The other is that, as a general rule, financial assets (being denominated in money terms) will be more liquid than real assets. Hence, they will be better substitutes for money than real assets. Let us now consider the relationships among liabilities and assets of different groups of participants in financial markets.

2.5 PARTICIPANTS IN FINANCIAL MARKETS

We shall consider briefly five groups of participants in financial markets: the Bank of England, commercial banks, other financial institutions, firms producing goods and services, and households.

2.5.1 The Bank of England

The Bank of England will be dealt with in more detail in Chapter 3. Here there are only two points we need make. The first is that two of the principal liabilities of the Bank (notes and coin; and the bankers' balances held by the clearing banks to enable the clearing system to work) are part of almost all available measures of money. The second is that the Bank, in its role of manager of the government's debt, has to organise new issues of government debt, bearing in mind the maturity dates of existing government liabilities. Decisions about this may affect relationships among interest rates on financial assets of different maturities (the so-called term structure of interest rates). More generally, the way in which government debt is financed can have important consequences for other participants in financial markets.

2.5.2 Commercial banks

In our earlier discussion of money, we pointed out that bank deposits are money. Deposits are liabilities of banks and are matched by bank assets, largely in the form of loans. It is possible, then, to think of bank lending as being a major determinant of the size of the money supply. Here we are talking about total loans by banks (or net indebtedness to banks). At any time, new loans will be being made and old loans will be being repaid. It is only when the new loans are greater in value than the repayments being made that bank deposits and, hence, the money supply will increase in value. Later, when we talk of new bank lending adding to the size of the money stock, we are assuming new lending greater in amount than current repayments.

Banks must also arrange their portfolios of assets in line with the nature of their liabilities and will be constantly seeking to trade-off liquidity against the higher rates of return usually available on less liquid assets.

It is worth pointing out here that in our earlier discussion of the role of banks in the creation of money we were referring only to clearing banks, because it is the clearing system which effectively turns bank deposits into money. However, there are some hundreds of other commercial banks which participate indirectly in the clearing system by holding deposits with clearing banks. As we shall see, the deposits of these banks are also included in most official measures of the money supply.

This has two important practical consequences. Firstly, since the distinction between banks and other financial institutions is by no means clear-cut, an arbitrary element enters into official measures of the money supply which does not exist in theoretical discussions based only on the clearing system.

Secondly, official measures will obviously have a degree of double-counting since a small part of any deposit with a non-clearing bank will also become a deposit with a clearing bank and be counted twice. This, in turn, means that shifts of deposits from clearing banks to other banks or from non-clearing banks to other (perhaps very similar) financial institutions will affect the official measures of the money supply. Given such things, it is bound to be the case that attempts to find a stable link between measures of the money supply and expenditure will take the form of trial and error.

2.5.3 Other financial institutions

Many other types of organisation participate in financial markets. Collectively these are frequently referred to as non-bank financial intermediaries (NBFIs). They include building societies, hire purchase companies, life assurance companies and pension funds. They, too, must match their assets and liabilities in respect of their maturities.

In this regard, it is worth considering the importance to such institutions of expectations about future interest rates. We have shown in Chapter 1 that the price people will be prepared to pay for financial assets will vary inversely with the rate of interest. However, the amount of variation will depend on the maturity date of the asset in question – the further away that date is, the more important will be the current market interest rate in the decision as to what price to pay for the asset. This is because the face value of the asset to be repaid on maturity is of much less significance for a long-dated asset than for a short-dated asset.

Consider a £100 bond which is due to mature in two months' time. The price a person will be prepared to pay for it will not vary much from £100 no matter what happens to current market interest rates; but changes in interest rates will be crucial to the price paid for a similar bond which is not due to mature until the year 2000. After all, the present value of a promise to pay £100 in fifteen years' time is not very great.

This means that if a financial institution thinks that interest rates are going to rise in the future, its judgement about the relative attractiveness of short-dated and long-dated financial assets will change. It will wish to hold more of its assets in shorter dated form; that is, it will wish to move its portfolio of assets in the direction of greater liquidity. Part of this decision may well involve holding more money than previously. This decision may have implications for firms which are seeking long-term loans.

2.5.4 Firms producing goods and services

The assets of firms consist of physical assets (plant and machinery, buildings, work-in-progress, inventories of goods and raw materials) and financial assets including notes and coin and deposits with financial institutions. The present value of their plant and machinery will be closely related to their expected future sales and to market interest rates. Their decisions to increase the size of their capital stock (to invest) will also depend on such things.

The liabilities of firms consist of the value of shares in the company (equity), bonds and debentures issued to the public, and loans from financial institutions, including loans from banks in the form of overdrafts. A decision to invest may mean simply a change in the composition of assets, e.g. a firm sells financial assets acquired through retaining past profits and buys additional machinery with the proceeds. Many investment decisions, however, involve an increase in assets and, consequently, in one or more forms of liabilities.

Thus, a firm can finance investment through new share issues. This is an attractive avenue for firms since no fixed repayments are implied. Dividends will need to be paid to keep shareholders happy, but dividends can be related to the current profit performance of the company. This method of raising funds may not be available, however, since it depends on the willingness of existing shareholders and others to buy the new shares. The market may well have a different opinion of the firm's future prospects than its management has.

An alternative is to seek long-term loans. This allows the matching of liabilities with the newly acquired illiquid physical assets. However, long-term loans may not seem attractive to lenders (for example, if they think interest rates will soon rise). On the other hand, if firms think interest rates may fall in the future, they may not wish to borrow for long periods. To do so might mean that a firm is saddled with a twenty-year loan at a rate of interest of, say, 16 per cent when current market rates of interest have fallen to, perhaps, 12 per cent.

Finally, firms may take shorter term loans from banks. This provides greater flexibility of interest rates (possibly a considerable advantage in times of great uncertainty about future interest rates), but increases the risk that a firm's assets may become too illiquid to meet repayments on its liabilities. Remember, if firms increase their bank overdrafts, the money supply rises in size. Thus, the decisions of firms to invest or not, and the decisions as to how to raise the funds needed for investment, are both important in determining the size of the money supply.

2.5.5 Households

Households are, in the aggregate, net savers. Many households, however, are net borrowers. They, too, will need to match maturities of assets and liabilities. Assets will include expected future earnings (human wealth). These are not at all liquid. Consequently, the higher the proportion of a household's wealth which is in the form of human wealth, the more likely it is that the household will balance its asset portfolio by holding some very liquid assets (including money).

Consider the case of someone with a mortgage. Regular repayments must be made. Suppose that the person's principal asset is expected future earnings; then the threat of redundancy looms. It may well seem sensible in these circumstances to hold savings in a liquid form to guarantee that the mortgage repayments can be met when they fall due.

As with firms, decisions of households regarding the amount of their borrowing and the form of that borrowing will have implications for the size of the money supply.

2.6 MONETARISTS, KEYNESIANS AND DEFINITIONS OF MONEY

Because Keynesians have always tended to look at money from the liquidity preference point of view, they have been inclined to argue that it is very difficult to say which financial assets should be regarded as money and which not. They have argued that wherever the dividing line is drawn, money and other financial assets can be regarded as good substitutes for each other. The only clear demarcation is between financial assets and real assets, which are seen as poor substitutes for each other. Further, since it is difficult to know what to count as money, no great faith should be put in any particular measure of money. Consequently, there is little point in basing an economic policy on an attempt to keep under control the rate of growth of such a measure.

A corollary of the foregoing is that because there are several types of very liquid assets, it will be relatively easy for banks and other financial institutions to switch among assets and to maintain their ability to lend in the face of government attempts to restrict it. Thus, even if a government knew which monetary aggregate it should be controlling, it would not be able to achieve the necessary control.

Monetarists, on the other hand, concentrate on the use of money in the purchase of commodities and feel that it is possible to draw a clear-cut line between it and all other assets. The trick then becomes to find a practical measure of the money supply which has a stable relationship with the level of expenditure in the economy **and** which can be controlled by the government. It becomes, as monetarists are fond of saying, simply an empirical question.

Another way of expressing the difference is in terms of the velocity of money. Monetarists believe that a measure of the money supply which will give a constant or predictable velocity of circulation can be found. Then, we may be uncertain as to how long control of this aggregate will take to have its effect on expenditure and then on the rate of inflation, but we will be confident that in the long run this control will have the desired effect.

Keynesians believe that the velocity of any monetary aggregate is going to be variable and, indeed, that the very act of controlling it will lead to changes in velocity. The implication is that changes in the money supply induce people to change the quantity of money they are willing to hold. To try to resolve this issue we need to look in some detail at both the supply of and the demand for money.

QUESTIONS

Essay questions

1. Select one of the sentences below which you think shows the clearest appreciation of the functions of money. Explain the reasons for your selection.

   (a) 'We can't afford the money to pay for the Channel Tunnel.'

(b) 'I keep my money in stocks and shares.'

(c) If I didn't keep cash in my pocket or a cheque book handy I would always be running to the bank before I could buy a packet of cigarettes.' (JMB)

2. What is money? Explain what acts as money in the UK at present. (JMB)

3. What is the relationship between 'wealth' and 'money'? What are the major problems involved in providing a precise definition of 'wealth'?

4. Explain the terms 'active balances' and 'idle balances'. Why might anyone wish to hold money as an idle balance?

Discussion questions

1. Which of the following do you think might reasonably be regarded as money?

   Deposits with the National Giro; credit cards; building society deposits; cheque books; cheque-guarantee cards; notes and coin held in bank vaults; National Savings accounts; Brian Robson.

   Try to think of things which might confuse other students as to whether or not they might reasonably be thought of as 'money'.

2. What is meant by liquidity? Consider the degree of liquidity of the following assets:

   Government stock maturing in the year 2000; a warehouse full of space-invader games; gold bullion; a building society deposit; a parcel of shares of the National Westminster Bank; Derby County's football ground.

   List as many other assets as you can think of and consider the liquidity of each.

3. List as many types of non-bank financial intermediaries (NBFI$_5$) as you can. What basically do they do?

4. Try to find out as much as you can about the operation of a clearing bank and of a building society. Consider the ways in which they are (a) similar, (b) different.

FURTHER READING

The standard treatment of the nature and uses of money is widely available and is included in Crockett (1979), Vane and Thompson (1982) and Lipsey (1983), though many books tend simply to classify and to list features rather than to explain what money is. Few books attempt to deal with basic questions which trouble students.

It is usually also taken for granted that students know what economists mean by 'wealth'. Exceptions include Parkin and Bade (1982) Ch. 4. The notion of 'liquidity' is, however, dealt with in many books, one of which is Rowan (1983) Ch. 22. The different attitudes of monetarists and Keynesians to money is explained everywhere, though not often at a level accessible to beginning students. Detailed treatments from different perspectives include Dow and Earl (1982), Vane and Thompson (1979) and Morgan (1978). Most general macroeconomic texts at second-year undergraduate level explain monetarist and Keynesian approaches. One such book is Challen *et al.* (1984).

3

THE SUPPLY OF MONEY

3.1 THE OFFICIAL MEASURES OF MONEY

The uncertainty we have just discussed, surrounding the nature of money and how it works, poses an obvious problem for the conduct of policy. Provided we think that money has any relevance at all to expenditure and thus to output, employment and prices, we need some way of recording what is happening to the money stock. At this point we may say theory is confronted by reality: something has to be measured. In the UK, the Bank of England collects and publishes data on the size of the money stock, defined in various ways. Table 3.1 summarises these definitions and the relationships between them.

Starting at the top of the table, the **wide monetary base** is composed of notes and coin (in circulation and with the banks) together with the balances ('bankers' balances') which banks themselves hold at the Bank of England for operational purposes. As we shall see in the next section, the supply of this cash and balances is ultimately a constraint upon the quantity of deposits which banks can safely create. For this reason, some have argued that if the authorities were to control the 'base', they would automatically control deposits and in a way which is much more direct and effective than the methods currently used. Section 4.1 explores more fully the method of monetary base control and the difficulties confronting it.

In November 1983 the wide monetary base first received some publicity when the Chancellor of the Exchequer announced that the government was considering giving more attention to this very narrow definition of money as a possible substitute for the existing narrow measure, M_1. The argument is that M_1 (see below) has come in recent years to contain increasing quantities of interest-bearing deposits, the demand for which is obviously influenced by changes in interest rates. As a measure of that part of the money stock held purely for transactions purposes, it has something to commend it (after all, notes and coin, which make up 91 per cent of the wide monetary base, would hardly be used for any other purpose). Even so, it has possible rivals in the slightly wider measures, non-interest-bearing M_1 (NIBM$_1$) and M_2. Because the wide monetary base is a narrower measure of money than M_1, it is sometimes referred to as **M_0**. In his March 1984 budget the Chancellor announced that in future the target rate of growth for M_1 would be replaced by a target rate for M_0.

Next in Table 3.1, we come to a well-known measure of the money stock, M_1, sometimes referred to as the 'narrow' definition of money. M_1 includes notes and coin in circulation with the non-bank private sector together with the total of its sterling sight deposits with institutions in the monetary sector. In the first quarter of 1983, M_1 stood at £41 328 m., consisting of £11 956 m. of notes and coin and £29 372 m. of sight deposits.

In an argument about the relevance of money to expenditure, the case for a measure of money stock such as M_1 is overwhelming. Notes and coin are used exclusively as a means of payment, and sight deposits (given that they include cheque-book supporting current accounts which are used similarly) are also central to the exchange and payment process. Nonetheless, there are two defects of M_1 as a measure of means of payment in the UK economy. The first is that some private sector sight deposits are large and interest bearing. These deposits (over £100 000 for purposes of classification) are usually deposits made by firms and are best thought of as short-term investments or 'wholesale' deposits. It is unlikely that variation in their size (and therefore in the size of M_1) tells us anything useful about changes in the supply of means of payment. The other weakness of M_1 is that it **excludes** all private sector interest-bearing time deposits. However, some of these – especially those where the notice required is less than one month – can quite readily be converted into means of payment. Therefore, if what we want is an accurate measure of readily available means of payment, we could usefully throw out of M_1 the wholesale interest-bearing sight deposits and bring in from sterling M_3 the small (those less than £100 000) short-term deposits. If we also add building society deposits with less that one month to maturity and deposits in the National Savings Bank ordinary account, this gives us a measure of 'retail' deposits,

Table 3.1 Relationships among the monetary and liquidity aggregates and their components

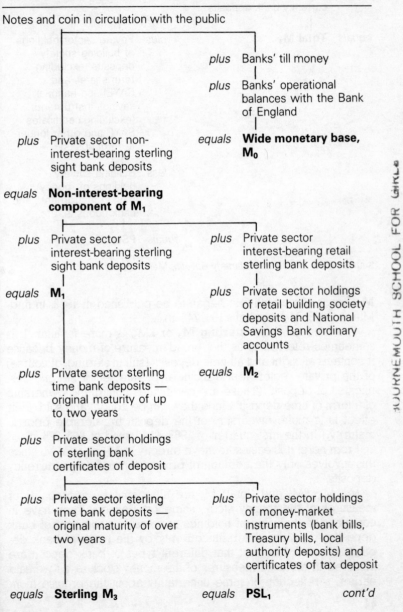

Notes and coin in circulation with the public

plus Banks' till money

plus Banks' operational balances with the Bank of England

plus Private sector non-interest-bearing sterling sight bank deposits   *equals* **Wide monetary base, M_0**

equals **Non-interest-bearing component of M_1**

plus Private sector interest-bearing sterling sight bank deposits   *plus* Private sector interest-bearing retail sterling bank deposits

equals **M_1**

plus Private sector holdings of retail building society deposits and National Savings Bank ordinary accounts

plus Private sector sterling time bank deposits — original maturity of up to two years   *equals* **M_2**

plus Private sector holdings of sterling bank certificates of deposit

plus Private sector sterling time bank deposits — original maturity of over two years   *plus* Private sector holdings of money-market instruments (bank bills, Treasury bills, local authority deposits) and certificates of tax deposit

equals **Sterling M_3**   *equals* **PSL_1**   *cont'd*

plus Private sector foreign
currency bank deposits

|

equals **Total M₃**　　　　　*plus* Private sector holdings
of building society
deposits (excluding
term shares and
SAYE) and national
savings instruments
(excluding certificates,
SAYE and other longer-
term deposits)

|

less Building society
holdings of money-
market instruments and
bank deposits, etc.

|

equals **PSL₂**

Source: *Bank of England Quarterly Bulletin,* March 1984

M_2, figures for which first began to be published in 1982. In mid-March 1983, M_2 stood at £105 745 m.

The next measure, **sterling M_3** or £M_3, is more familiar. It is sometimes referred to as the 'broad' measure of money because it contains all sight and all time deposits (still in sterling, of course) of the private sector. It also includes private sector sterling certificates of deposit. (These are certificates confirming ownership of a form of time deposit. Since they can be bought and sold, their effect is to make ownership of the deposit transferable prior to maturity.) In the first quarter of 1983, £M_3 stood at £96 325 m.

From here, it is easiest to move directly to **M_3**, or total M_3 since this involves only the addition of private sector foreign currency deposits.

M_1, M_2, £M_3 and (total) M_3 are all 'monetary' aggregates or measures of the money stock, somehow defined. They have in common the inclusion of holdings of notes and coin and of bank deposits. They are differentiated only by the types of bank deposit included. The fact that different types of bank deposit are included in different measures of the money stock is, as we said earlier, a reflection of some uncertainty about the precise monetary factors that influence people's expenditure plans. Is it currently available means of payment such as cheque-book supporting sight deposits, or the knowledge that such means of payment could be obtained at tolerable cost when required? If it is the former, then what happens to M_1 and M_2 is plainly important. If it is the latter, then at the very least we need to consider the behaviour of £M_3.

We stressed in Section 2.2.3 that a building society deposit itself is not a means of payment. Using such a deposit to pay a bill involves either withdrawing cash from the society or taking a cheque **drawn on the building society's bank**. The means of payment acceptable to the presenter of the bill is, once again, a claim on a sight deposit with a bank, that deposit being in the name of the building society. The fact that some societies now issue cheque-books makes no difference to this point; it merely increases the (already considerable) convenience of a building society deposit as an interest-bearing near substitute for 'real' money. In effect, the managers of the society in question are delegating to certain customers the right to sign cheques drawn on the society's bank account.

The recognition that in recent years there has been a rapid growth of financial assets which are not themselves money but by being very near substitutes have added to liquidity and therefore possibly to expenditure, has led to the recent compilation and publication of 'private sector liquidity' aggregates, **PSL**$_1$ and **PSL**$_2$ alongside the better known monetary aggregates. A glance at Table 3.1 reveals that while these aggregates may be loosely thought of as 'broader' than £M_3, there is more involved than the mere addition of assets to the £M_3 list. First of all, because the PSL aggregates are concerned with private sector liquidity, all public sector deposits are excluded and, as a recognition of our earlier point that not all bank deposits are particularly liquid, private sector time deposits originally made for a period of two years or over are also excluded. To the remaining items of £M_3 we add a variety of money market instruments to get PSL$_1$ and then the more liquid types of building society deposit and national savings instrument. Lastly, for completeness, we should note that since building societies are themselves part of the private sector their holdings of financial assets, such as bank deposits, will be included every time private sector holdings of such assets are included in any aggregate. If we then include (as in PSL$_2$) private sector holdings of building society deposits – some proportion of which represents a claim upon building society deposits with banks – we should be double-counting and these are therefore excluded.

3.2 THE PROLIFERATION OF OFFICIAL MEASURES

The list of money and liquidity aggregates **monitored** by the authorities has grown with the passage of time. Within that list of monitored aggregates a similar process has been at work with those chosen as targets. For example, from 1976 to 1981, governments announced target rates of growth for $£M_3$ alone. In 1982, M_1 and PSL_2 were added to the list. In March 1984, M_1 was replaced by M_0 and PSL_2 was dropped. The proliferation of measures and their monitoring can always be welcomed as an attempt to have more information about monetary conditions. To explain the changing fashions among targets, however, we have to consider in more detail the arguments behind their announcement. The starting point, as we said at the end of the last chapter, is that if the velocity of circulation is stable (or at least changes only slowly and predictably over time) then confining the growth of money supply (M_s) within a target range must confine the growth of PT. Thus, any definition of the money stock for targeting purposes must satisfy two conditions in order to be successful. Firstly, its velocity has to be stable; that is to say, if we perform the calculation

$$\frac{\text{GDP (in money terms)}}{M_s}$$

for a number of years, the result should be constant or growing at a steady rate. Secondly, the definition of M_s has also to be one which the authorities can, in practical terms, control.

It has to be said of all the aggregates that none of them shows the consistent stability of velocity which its use as a target ideally requires. $£M_3$ has shown very sharp fluctuations, in the early 1970s and again since its adoption as a target in 1976. Interestingly, its unstable history was known at the time of its adoption and it was recognised that M_1, whose velocity was comparatively stable, might for this reason be a better choice. It was rejected at the time, however, because it was easier in $£M_3$ to trace the apparent effect of changes in borrowing which were themselves sources of monetary growth – the Public Sector Borrowing Requirement, bank lending, government debt sales, etc. (These connections are explored in Section 4.2.) Since its adoption as a target in 1982, the velocity of M_1 has fallen below its trend rate of growth, possibly because the growing tendency of banks to pay interest on certain types of M_1 deposit has moved M_1 towards a form of holding wealth and away from its role primarily as a medium of exchange. In consequence, the community has become willing to hold a greater quantity in relation to the level of expenditure it intends to carry out. Hence, as we saw above, there is an argument for the replacement of M_1 by some yet narrower aggregate.

The arithmetic of velocity and the demand for money is easy to understand. So, too, are the sorts of institutional changes that might bring about departures from trend. If banks start to pay interest on M_1 balances they become more attractive to hold, and velocity falls; as the use of credit cards spreads, a given quantity of money (however defined) can now support a greater quantity of transactions, and velocity rises. The worry about changing velocities is not that they need explaining but that the explanation may have something to do with the very fact of their being chosen as targets for control purposes. If this is the case, then choosing a target on the basis of past stable velocity is the very cause of future instability.

This is one version of Goodhart's Law: 'to control is to distort'. Suppose, for illustration, that $£M_3$ is the target, chosen because of its hitherto stable relation to money expenditure and that confining it within a growth range requires cuts in government spending to reduce the growth of the public sector's contribution. Further, suppose that the cuts in spending involve reductions in aid to industry, and firms respond by increasing their borrowing from non-bank financial intermediaries. To attract deposits to meet the demand from firms, NBFIs have to raise interest rates to attract new deposits. Nothing has happened to the money stock; $£M_3$ is still on course. If the rise in interest rates succeeds in attracting deposits, it does so by persuading some people to economise on their money holdings and lend to firms. Velocity has risen to finance the expenditure firms were determined to undertake, and the relationship between $£M_3$ and expenditure has changed.

Although it does not establish the validity of 'Goodhart's Law', it is worth noting that velocity has proved most stable over the years for (a) very narrow measures such as M_0 and notes and coin which, far from being the subject of control, have actually been supplied on demand, and also for (b) PSL_2 which, because of its very breadth, authorities find difficult to control. It is probably too cynical to see the frequent emergence of new targets as confirming the failure of their predecessors, but there is certainly a difficulty in finding one whose stability will survive its control.

3.3 THE MONETARY SECTOR

To understand how money is created, and more especially to appreciate methods and difficulties of monetary control, we need some acquaintance with the institutional framework within which the process takes place.

At the very simplest level, we need to think of a 'monetary sector' which is controlled, or at least influenced, by the 'monetary authorities'. In the UK the monetary authorities comprise the Treasury and the Bank of England. Broadly speaking, the Treasury decides upon the objectives of monetary policy and the Bank is responsible for the day to day selection and operation of various instruments designed to achieve these objectives. Thus, the Treasury might decide upon a target rate of monetary growth or a level of interest rates or exchange rate. The Bank would then decide upon the timing, quantity and maturity of bill and bond sales or changes in reserve requirements necessary to bring these about. Like all general statements, this is a simplification. The Bank will at times express a view about the wisdom and feasibility of certain monetary objectives just as the Treasury will have a preference for ways of achieving them, but there is enough realism here to make the generalisation useful.

The 'monetary sector' has its origin in the Banking Act of 1979 which placed upon the Bank of England a statutory obligation to supervise, for the protection of depositors, a number of institutions which accept deposits from the public. The institutions in question were to be known collectively as the 'monetary sector', which includes the clearing banks and other institutions recognised as banks under the 1979 Act. Also included are the discount houses, the trustee savings banks, the National Girobank, the banking department of the Bank of England and a large number of licensed (in pursuance of the 1979 Act) deposit-taking institutions. In August 1981 the 'monetary sector' replaced what had been known as the 'banking sector' for purposes of monetary control.

In Chapter 2 we defined money as notes and coin in circulation with the non-bank private sector together with bank deposits. It is important to recognise a number of points about this definition.

Firstly, the 'bank deposits' in question are deposits with any institution belonging to the monetary sector. Henceforth, unless otherwise specified, a reference to 'banks' will mean 'institutions comprising the monetary sector'.

Secondly, although we might argue about the exact list of various types of bank deposit to be included (sight and time, sterling and overseas, public and private sector) this definition is very close to the narrowest practicable definition of money. Although some economists might argue for the inclusion of other assets in certain circumstances, no-one argues for the **exclusion** of bank deposits. Whenever we think of money, therefore, we are bound to think of bank deposits of some description.

Thirdly, bank deposits dominate the money stock; for example, in March 1984, bank deposits made up over 70 per cent of M_1 and over 87 per cent of $\pounds M_3$.

Fourthly, it follows from the dominance of bank deposits that the behaviour of banks – that is, in creating or destroying bank deposits – will be quantitatively of great significance in the monetary expansion/contraction process. For this reason, we need to look a little more closely at the position and function of institutions within the monetary sector.

3.3.1 Banks

Banks are private sector institutions with responsibilities to their shareholders for efficient and profitable operation. Over the years they have developed a wide range of services such as insurance, tax advice, executor and trustee services, credit cards and unit trusts all in the, generally correct, belief that these would be welcomed by customers and profitable to the shareholders. It is important to remember, however, that their main and traditional functions – operating a payments transmission system and providing short-term personal and commercial loans – are also carried out with strictly commercial aims in view. None of this is meant to suggest that banks are ruthless profit maximisers; indeed the banker–client relationship is a complex one which, in times of severe monetary constraint, banks have sometimes sought to maintain even at the cost of some loss of profit on marginal business. What it does emphasise, however, is that banks have quite different objectives from those of the monetary authorities and that there will be times when these interests conflict. Banks make profits by, among other things, making loans which add to the money supply. We must not be surprised, therefore, that banks and their customers are not often on the side of the monetary authorities and that effective monetary controls are not easy to devise. A glance at Table 3.2 makes clearer the relevance of this profit orientation to the money supply process.

Table 3.2 Sterling Assets and Liabilities of the Monetary Sector Summary of Monthly Reporting Institutions mid-November 1983

	£m.		% of total sterling liabilities
Sterling liabilities			
Deposits: sight	45 108		24.6
time	99 762		54.4
certificates of deposit	9 812		5.4
Total		154 712	84.4
Other		28 577	15.6
Total		183 289	100.0
Sterling assets			
Notes and coin	1 676		0.9
Operational balances at the Bank of England	196		0.1
Loans to the London discount market	5 109		2.8
Other market loans	47 145		25.7
Bills	3 306		1.8
Other government securities	6 611		3.6
Loans and advances	99 339		54.2
Other	20 075		10.9
		183 457	100.0

Note: Assets and liabilities do not balance owing to the exclusion of non-sterling assets and liabilities.

Source: *Bank of England Quarterly Bulletin*, Dec. 1983, Table 3.1

On the liabilities side, the balance sheet is dominated by customers' deposits. These deposits – a major constituent of the money stock, remember – are a liability to a bank because they may be withdrawn, as notes and coin, or transferred to a customer of another bank, or transferred, as we shall see later, out of the banking system altogether as a payment to the government's account at the Bank of England. At all times banks must be ready to meet all such withdrawals or transfers their customers wish to make.

On some of these deposits banks will be paying interest, and this, together with the cost of providing cheque-book and clearing facilities, is part of the banks' operating costs. To cover these costs and to make a profit, banks use these deposits to acquire earning assets. In deciding the distribution of their asset holdings, banks have therefore to bear in mind two considerations usually expressed as 'liquidity' and 'profitability'. By 'profitability' we mean a flow of earnings and/or capital gain from an asset which exceeds the cost of acquiring and holding that asset. By 'liquidity' we mean the ability to exchange the asset for money, quickly and for a capital sum which is reasonably certain. The first of these principles obviously arises from what we have said regarding banks' profit-making activities; the second arises from the nature of their liabilities. Most bank deposits can be withdrawn on demand or at very short notice and, as we noted above, it is absolutely essential that a bank should be known to be able to meet its obligations.

In Table 3.2, 'loans and advances' to borrowers who pay interest are among the banks' highest earning assets and the search for profitability explains their domination of the asset side of the balance sheet. The need to hold other, generally poorer earning, assets is explained by the need for liquidity. Moving to the other end of the asset spectrum, notes, coin and balances with the Bank of England earn nothing for a bank but are essential in some quantity because it is with these that banks meet customers' demands for withdrawals and transfers. On the face of it, this degree of perfect liquidity perhaps looks perilously small. In November 1983, cash and balances amounted to less than half of one per cent of total deposit liabilities and only 1.2 per cent of sterling deposit liabilities. The fact that banks can afford to have so small a proportion of total assets ready to meet withdrawals is partly explained by the banks' experience and skill and partly by the statistical fact of the very large numbers of deposits and withdrawals which they handle producing very stable aggregate behaviour on the part of their customers. Experience has taught banks that the rate of withdrawal and rate of acquisition of new deposits is a small and fairly stable proportion of existing deposits, and that on any particular day an individual bank is likely to receive deposits and face withdrawals which roughly cancel each other out.

Because they are held for the purpose of meeting customers' withdrawals and for making payments on behalf of customers to recipients with accounts at other banks, these balances are often termed 'prudential balances' and it is assumed that banks wish to hold a minimum level – normally a proportion of existing deposits – to ensure adequate liquidity. We shall see below that maintaining adequate prudential balances is an important constraint on the expansion of deposits.

The small proportion of 'cash' to deposits is also explained by some of the other assets in the banks' portfolios. Loans to the London discount market are funds lent out by the banks but are repayable on demand. This is not quite so liquid as the banks' own balances at the Bank of England but it is a very close substitute which has the added advantage that it earns a rate of interest. Moving along the scale a little further, government securities are less liquid; there is a ready market on which they can be sold quickly if banks have to raise cash unexpectedly, but the realisable capital value may be a little uncertain. There is always the possibility of having to sell at a loss against the price at which they were originally bought. Certainly, if several banks try to sell securities simultaneously the price is likely to be driven down from the existing market price; and similarly with other assets in the balance sheet. They are held in total in order to provide what banks think is the optimal mix of profitability and liquidity. The fact that so few perfectly liquid assets (notes and coin and balances at the Bank of England) are held has to be seen in the light of the relatively high liquidity of a number of other assets which, nonetheless, yield a positive return.

What we have just been describing are the factors (liquidity and profitability) which determine the optimum or equilibrium distribution of banks' assets. From this it follows that, given an equilibrium position, a change in the profitability or liquidity of any asset will produce an adjustment in the holdings of all assets until a new equilibrium is achieved. Conversely, an equilibrium position which is upset by a change in the quantity of an asset available to banks – the profitability and liquidity of the asset being unchanged – will see banks trying to restore their original position. Equipped with some elementary knowledge of banks' balance sheets, we are now in a position to appreciate the way in which banks' commercial behaviour can affect the money stock and we can see some of the constraints upon that behaviour.

To do this, we shall use a simplified balance sheet (see Tables 3.3, 3.4 and 3.5); that is, simplified compared with Table 3.2 in the range of assets and liabilities listed, not in the principles we have just been discussing. We also concentrate for the moment on the behaviour of an individual bank (see Table 3.3), moving to the aggregate case later.

Now let us suppose that in the conduct of its day-to-day business our hypothetical bank is presented with two situations, both of which illustrate how deposits and the money stock may change

Table 3.3 A simplified balance sheet (1)

Liabilities		Assets	
Deposits	100	Balances at the Bank of England	10
		Money at call	20
		Securities	20
		Loans and advances	50
Total	100	Total	100

Ratio of balances to deposits = 10%

Table 3.4 A simplified balance sheet (2)

Liabilities		Assets	
Deposits (old)	100	Balances at the Bank of England	10
Deposits (new)	10	Money at call	20
Deposits (new)	10	Securities	30
		Loans and advances	60
Total	120	Total	120

Ratio of balances to deposits = 8.3%

(see Table 3.4).One customer sells some government securities to the bank and another applies for and receives a loan.

The customers' accounts (their deposits) have been credited with, respectively, the bank's payment for the securities (10) and the loan (10) and the money stock has increased in consequence (by 20). Note, however, that the bank's balance sheet, its assets and liabilities, still balances because on the asset side it has acquired extra securities (10) and extra loans (10). On the perfectly reasonable assumption that the newly acquired assets earn interest in excess of maintaining the new liabilities, the bank's profits will also have increased. On the face of it, actions which increase the money stock also increase bank profits. Has banking become a licence to print money?

Fortunately, from the authorities' point of view, there are some constraints and it is in the promotion and discouragement of these constraints that hope for the authorities lies.

First of all, banks cannot increase their lending unless people wish to borrow. The bank in our illustration increased its deposits by 10 because a customer took out or increased a loan facility. On his use of that loan he will have to pay interest and that is a cost which will be incurred only if the expenditure which is contemplated yields a rate of return which promises at least to cover the cost of the interest payments. In other words, for a given level of bank interest rates, the demand for loans will depend upon the prospects for profitable business investment and on the rate of interest charged by other lenders. Of course, in a situation where the demand for bank credit is low, banks could attempt to stimulate it by lowering interest rates, but if that in turn means lowering the rates paid to depositors they may find deposits draining away to other institutions and this, as we shall see, imposes a constraint of a different kind.

In addition to the demand for loans, the demand for deposits is also a constraint upon the banks' ability to expand the money supply. By the demand for deposits we mean the willingness of the non-bank public to hold their wealth in the form of money as opposed to other types of financial or even non-financial assets. In our illustration a customer received a bank deposit in exchange for an alternative asset, a government security. The public's willingness to make this exchange and to hold money as an asset will depend upon their preferences, the rate of return on bank deposits relative to other types of asset and possibly on anticipated changes in their relative rates of return.

Thirdly, in creating new customer deposits our hypothetical bank has to face the possibility that some or all of these new deposits will be withdrawn to make payments to people who hold accounts with other banks. Although there may be occasions when customers acquire bank deposits by taking out interest-bearing loans or selling interest-earning assets in order to hold idle balances, we should normally expect them to do so in order to spend. If customers make withdrawals to pay people with accounts at other banks, then our original bank will have to transfer an equal amount of balances at the Bank of England to the bank of the person who receives the payment. Again, the balance sheet balances, but now new deposits have been partially run down and the corresponding asset adjustment is the loss of bankers' balances. Whereas our bank began by holding a 10 per cent ratio of prudential balances (in Table 3.3), this has fallen in Table 3.5 to just over 5 per cent.

So far we have illustrated the deposit expansion/contraction process by reference to an individual bank, but, of course, when we speak of a monetary expansion/contraction we have in mind the behaviour of a large number of banks acting in a similar way. In moving from the individual to the aggregate case we have to modify our view of the process, in particular with respect to the last constraint we have just been discussing. If an individual bank expands its deposits it is quite likely that it will see a large proportion of them transferred to other banks. It would be a strange, not to say fortuitous, coincidence if the recipients of the new deposits used them to facilitate exchange only with other customers of the same bank. However, if the whole of the banking system

Table 3.5 A simplified balance sheet (3)

Liabilities		Assets	
Deposits (old)	100	Balances at the	
Deposits (new)	8	Bank of England	6
Deposits (new)	8	Money at call	20
		Securities	30
		Loans	60
Total	116	Total	116

Ratio of balances to deposits = 5.2%

were expanding its deposits, as would be the case with an increase in the money supply, might it not be argued that the actions of millions of individual customers would be largely self-cancelling? That is to say, although bank A would see its newly created deposits transferred in part to banks B, C and D, it would in return receive newly created deposits as the clients of B, C and D made payments to customers of bank A. **Net** transfers at the end of each day would be very small, and provided that all banks expanded their deposits at a roughly similar rate, then no individual bank would lose significant quantities of bankers' balances.

The answer is that it all depends upon the public's willingness to use the newly created deposits to make exchanges between clients of the clearing banks. This brings us to a central institutional feature of the British monetary system; namely, that the largest single supplier and purchaser of goods and services within the economy does not bank with the clearing banks at all. The government's accounts are at the Bank of England. Thus an increase in deposits which was used to make payments (for goods and services, for settlement of tax liabilities, for government bonds) drains bankers' balances from all banks simultaneously unless the government makes payment to the public (who deposit the funds with the clearing banks) in order to offset this drain. On a daily basis there are massive transfers of balances between the clearing banks' accounts at the Bank of England and the government's accounts. As we shall see in the next chapter, the monetary authorities' ability to nudge this flow in a particular direction in order to leave the banks with a net increase or decrease in their balances, is a potentially powerful source of influence over the banks' willingness and ability to create deposits.

There is one further group of institutions in the monetary sector whose role within the money supply process we need to understand. These are the discount houses, the ten members of the London Discount Market Association. The houses are 'the main market makers in bills' which means that they make a profit by buying and selling commercial and Treasury bills and that they do so on such a scale that the price of bills determined by their buying and selling activities strongly influences the price of bills held by other institutions. The bills in question are pieces of paper issued by the Treasury or commercial enterprises for a face value, say £50 000, at which they will be redeemed at some date in the future, normally ninety-one days from the day of issue. When they are issued and sold, however, they are sold 'at a discount', i.e. the buyer pays less than the face or redemption value. If a £50 000 bill is bought for £47 000 at the time of issue it is bought at a discount of 5 per cent which is the return that the purchaser will get when the bill is redeemed at face value in three months' time. Thus, although not strictly identical in numerical terms, a rate of discount may be likened to a rate of interest. Our 5 per cent discount on a three-month bill is equivalent to an annual compound rate of interest 22.8 per cent. The greater the discount at which bills trade, the higher the effective rate of interest they offer.

As the main buyers and holders of bills, the discount houses use money borrowed from the banks 'at call' – money that can be recalled instantly by the banks in case of need. Since this 'call money' carries a rate of interest, the arrangement is of mutual benefit to all parties. If the houses can buy bills at a discount which more than covers the interest payable on call money, they make a profit; at the same time, banks have a home for funds on which they earn interest and yet can recover, in case of emergency, at a moment's notice. From the banks' point of view, therefore, call money is an income earning first-line reserve asset after their balances held at the Bank of England.

It is their holding of banks' first-line reserve assets that brings the discount houses into the monetary control process, as we can appreciate if we return to the position we described above where the public is making payments to the government on a scale which results in a net transfer of bankers' balances to the government's accounts.

Finding their balances at the Bank of England reduced, the banks seek to restore the ratio of balances to deposits by retrieving money at call from the discount houses. To honour their obligations to the banks, the discount houses will have to liquidate quickly some part their bill holdings, and however this is done – by sales of the bills to the Bank of England or to other financial institutions – the result will be a fall in the price of bills, or, what amounts to the same thing, a rise in the rate of discount and the effective rate of interest. Knowing that bill rates are rising and that the houses will be willing to pay higher rates for call money to avoid the distress selling of bills, banks raise the rate charged on call money and, since call money is a near substitute for other bank assets, this will tend to raise short-term rates charged to other borrowers. If we bear in mind that the Bank of England is able to **encourage** a drain of balances from the banks (for example, by bond sales to the non-bank public), and that as the ultimate buyer of bills from the discount houses it can set the rate of discount at which it will be willing to buy those bills, we can appreciate the Bank of England's potential ability to influence banks' reserves and short-term interest rates.

Since constraining the quantity of bankers' balances may be expected to limit the banks' ability to expand deposits safely, and since a rise in interest rates may be expected to deter customers from wishing to expand overdrafts or to prefer holding bank deposits to interest earning assets, the institutional arrangements we have just described offer two distinct approaches to monetary control, and we shall be looking at these in Chapter 4.

3.4 CHANGES IN THE MONEY STOCK

In the last section we explored the principles underlying the banks' ability to create deposits and thereby add to the stock of money. The key points are worth repeating. Bank deposits, which form by far the largest part of banks' liabilities, are included in and dominate all the usual definitions of the money stock. A change in the total of bank deposits will, therefore, be reflected in a change in size of the money stock. Banks incur (create) liabilities in order to acquire assets (securities, call money, advances to customers), from holding which they make profit. Subject, therefore, to the limit imposed by the need to keep enough ready cash and balances at the Bank of England to meet day-to-day net withdrawals and transfers, the banks will wish to maximise their holdings of liabilities and assets – in other words, the size of their balance sheets.

In this section we are going to assume that banks are currently working within the limit imposed by the desired ratio of cash and balances to deposits (i.e. are free to expand their balance sheets) and we are going to look at five ways in which banks might be induced to increase their holdings of assets and liabilities and, hence, the money stock.

The first two possibilities are those that we used for illustration in the last section.

1. If a customer is granted overdraft facilities and uses them,

new deposits have been created. They have been created by the lending bank but they appear for the first time when our customer draws cheques on the facility and these cheques are paid into the recipient's bank, increasing the deposits in his name. The lending need not be in the form of an overdraft, of course; any form of bank lending will do. The aggressive marketing of personal loans (of fixed amount, interest rate and term) that we have seen in recent years works in the same way. By making the loans, banks have increased the total of deposits in the system (their liabilities) at the same time that they have acquired more earning assets (the interest-bearing loans).

2. The second case, it will be recalled, was where banks bought securities from the public. The simplest case to understand is where a bank buys securities from its own customer(s). Here, the purchase simply involves crediting an existing account with an increased balance. Once again, the bank has increased liabilities (the customer's enlarged deposit) and increased assets (the securities purchased). Seen from the customer's point of view, there has been an exchange of securities for money. That the money is 'new' money is best appreciated by asking the question: 'Whose deposits have been reduced in order to buy the securities?' If there were to be no overall increase in deposits it would have to be the case that purchasing the securities involved a **redistribution** – paying the seller by transferring deposits to his name from somewhere else in the system, as would happen, for example, if the securities were being bought by another member of the public. Clearly, that has not happened here. No one's deposits have been run down in order to pay for the securities. The bank has bought them by issuing a liability against itself and that liability happens to function as money. It has made, in effect, a promise to hold, transfer and, if required, convert into notes and coin a new sum of money on behalf of a customer. The creation of a deposit for the customer, which is what the promise amounts to, is a clear illustration that the bank has increased its liabilities, which it can do in any amount just like any other individual or firm. The crucial point, let us say once again, is that in this case the liability happens to be universally acceptable as money.

This is the simplest case in which the bank is involved in the purchase of securities. In practice, the process is usually more complicated since it is unlikely that a bank will often be making purchases from its own customers and crediting their accounts. More frequently a bank will be buying from organised markets in securities. Here, the bank's brokers will be buying from current holders of securities, the jobbers, to whom payment will have to be made. If the jobber happens to have an account at the purchasing bank, the account will be credited with the cost of the purchase, and the case is identical to that of the purchase from an ordinary customer of the bank. If, as is more likely to be the case, the jobber banks with another bank he will be paid by a cheque drawn on the purchasing bank which he will then pay into his own account. When cleared, this will involve a transfer of balances at the Bank of England from the purchasing bank to the jobber's bank. In this case, there has not been an expansion of the balance sheet because there has been no increase in the purchasing bank's deposits (the increase is in the jobber's bank). On the asset side, there has been no expansion either. Securities have been acquired (a gain) but balances at the Bank of England have been transferred from the purchasing bank (an equal loss). The balance sheet increase has taken place in the jobber's bank. It has his extra deposit (a liability) and the extra balance at the Bank of England (an asset) transferred from the purchasing bank. A new deposit has been created; the money stock has increased. If we add a little more realism still and assume that the market conditions which induce one bank to purchase extra holdings of securities are likely to encourage all banks similarly, then as each bank pays for its own purchases of securities by cheques paid into other banks, each will also be the recipient of new deposits created by the others.

3. There is a third set of circumstances, less frequently remarked on but similar in principle to the purchase of securities. This is the case where the bank buys goods and services from the non-bank public. Imagine, for example, the case where a bank decides to open premises in a town in which it currently has no branch. The premises will be bought from the seller, who, if he happens to have an account at the purchasing bank, will be credited with the purchase price of the premises. Bank liabilities have increased by the amount of the deposit credited to the seller/client. The asset side of the balance sheet has increased by the value of the premises acquired. The balance sheet and the money stock have expanded. Once again, this is easily appreciated if we ask: 'Whose deposit has been reduced in order to credit the seller?' No existing deposits have been reduced; there is no question of a transfer here. The bank has purchased the premises with a newly created deposit.

As with the securities purchase we can introduce the probability that the seller of the premises banks with another bank. He is paid with a cheque drawn on the purchasing bank which he then pays into his own. The purchasing bank has no increase in its own liabilities but neither has it an immediate increase in assets. The value of the premises acquired is offset by an equal transfer of balances at the Bank of England to the bank of the seller when his cheque is cleared. The increase in balance sheet size (and money stock) occurs in the seller's bank. It has increased deposits (liabilities) as a result of crediting his account with the value of the cleared cheque and increased assets in the form of expanded balances at the Bank of England as a result of the transfer from the purchasing bank. If, having bought the premises, the bank then pays a local building firm to convert them for banking use, the process will repeat itself.

4. The fourth set of circumstances surrounds the much more highly publicised issue of government borrowing. In what we might regard as the normal state of affairs where governments borrow from the non-bank public by selling government stock or persuading them to buy national savings instruments of one sort or another, there is plainly no increase in the money stock. The position is the same as if one member of the public were to lend to another. There is an exchange of money for a promise to repay with interest. Part of the money stock changes hands but there is no variation in the total.

However, just as it is possible for members of the non-bank public to borrow from each other or from the banking system, with quite different consequences for monetary growth, so it is possible for the government to do the same. The process is a little complicated, since there are three different ways it can be done.

(a) The first possibility is that the government borrows from the Bank of England by selling government securities to the Bank. In return the government's or, more strictly speaking, the public sector accounts at the Bank of England, are credited with funds to the value of the stock sold to the Bank. At this stage, nothing has happened to the balance sheets of the commercial banks but the balance sheet of the banking department of the Bank of England has been affected in the same way as that of the bank which, in our first case, purchased securities from a customer. The Bank of England has done precisely the same for its customer, the government.

61

Since the government is no more likely than a private individual to issue interest-bearing debt without a prior need to spend the proceeds, the process cannot rest here. The increased public sector deposits are spent on a wide variety of purchases of goods and services, the suppliers of which then pay the cheques drawn on the public sector accounts into their accounts with the commercial banks. At this point, the balance sheet expansion occurs. The banks increase their customers' deposits (liabilities) and present the cheques for payment to the Bank of England which credits the banks' balances at the Bank with an equal amount. It is important to note in passing that since the adjustment to the asset side of their balance sheets consists of a rise in balances held at the Bank of England, this form of government borrowing has increased not just the money stock but the overall liquidity position, strictly the monetary base, of the banking system. By increasing the ratio of balances to deposits, this method of government borrowing has eased the principal constraint on further bank lending and encouraged the possibility of a secondary expansion of deposits by any of the earlier processes we have described.

(b) Another possibility, still involving the sale of government securities, is that these are bought by the commercial banks themselves. Here we must remember our assumption at the beginning of this section that the banks were operating safely within the required cash and balances to deposits ratio because the purchase of the securities is going to mean initially a transfer from banks' balances to public sector deposits at the Bank of England. So far there is no increase in assets (though there has been a rearrangement of course – banks are now holding more government securities and fewer balances). Once again, however, the acquisition of funds by the government is only a preliminary to spending them. As the recipients deposit the cheques with their banks, the commercial banks gain liabilities (increased customer deposits) and, as the cheques are cleared, increased assets in the form of credits to their balances at the Bank of England. In short, the original level of balances is restored but on the asset side there has been a gain of government securities matched on the liabilities side by an equal increase in customers' deposits. The money stock has increased, of course, but it is worth noting, since we made the point in connection with the previous example, that balances having been restored to their original level the **ratio** of cash and balances to deposits has fallen. The liquidity position has deteriorated, bringing the monetary sector nearer to its safe limit. Further deposit expansion is less likely and, in this sense at least, the variation here described can be regarded as less expansionary than its predecessor.

(c) The last way in which government borrowing may have an impact on the money stock is where the government borrows directly from the Bank of England, with no sale or exchange of government securities taking place at all. From the monetary expansion point of view, the effect is similar to the first of these cases we looked at. The Bank of England has increased public sector deposits in the same way that a commercial bank increases deposits when it advances a loan. When the government spends its borrowing, the deposits of private sector recipients (banks' liabilities) are increased. On the asset side, when the cheques are cleared, the banks' balances at the Bank of England have risen by the amount of the government borrowing. Once again, as well as an increase in the money stock, we have an increase in the cash base and cash ratio which will permit further expansion of the money stock if the banks so wish. In the meantime, the increased cash holdings of the banks will be most likely placed at call in the discount market. This will increase the discount houses' demand for Treasury bills which the Bank will supply on behalf of the government. The proceeds of the sale are then used to pay off the original direct borrowing from the Bank. In effect, the government could be said to have financed its borrowing by the sale of Treasury bills but to appreciate the monetary implications of this process a clear distinction has to be made between the sale of government stock (the previous case) and the sale of Treasury bills. In the case of the sale of government stock to the banking system, deposits increased by the amount of the sale and this increase in liabilities was balanced by the acquisition of the stock as a (relatively illiquid) asset. In the case of Treasury bill finance, it has to be remembered that the purchase of the bills has been made with funds which would otherwise have appeared in the balance sheet as an excessive ratio of banks' balances to deposits. However, since the Bank of England stands always ready as lender of last resort to repurchase these bills from the discount houses in the event of the banks' retrieving their money at call, the bills are an extremely liquid asset. If banks so wish, they can always convert Treasury bill holdings to cash and bankers' balances which can then be used to finance further deposit creation.

5. The fifth and final source of a change in the money stock lies in the balance of payments. For the sake of consistency, we shall stay with the example of an increase in the money stock and this requires the assumption of a balance of payments surplus. In such circumstances, the demand for UK goods by overseas buyers exceeds the UK's demand for imports. If we assume for the moment that purchasers pay for the goods in their own currency, this means that at the current exchange rate the value of foreign exchange being received by UK suppliers exceeds the value of sterling being received by overseas suppliers. The UK recipients will present the foreign currency received to their banks for conversion to sterling. Again at the current exchange rate, since the inflow of foreign currency is greater than the outflow of sterling, the banks' supply of sterling to their customers must exceed the outflow to foreign suppliers. There has been a net increase in the sterling money stock.

It is customary, in discussion of the balance of payments and the money stock, to distinguish between the cases of fixed and floating exchange rate regimes. It should be appreciated, however, that this has no bearing on the circumstances so far described. If there is a surplus, there will be an increase in the domestic money stock whatever the exchange rate regime in operation. It may be argued that under freely floating exchange rates surpluses/deficits are less likely to emerge in the first place, but even this ignores the fact that, in practice, exchange rates do not float freely and countries continue to run surpluses/deficits; also, that exchange rates, if they adjust readily at all, do so in response to and not in anticipation of imbalances.

The exchange rate regime is relevant to the process outlined above in its subsequent course of events. The banks who receive the foreign exchange from their customers wanting sterling will eventually replenish their sterling holdings by buying sterling in the foreign exchange market with the foreign exchange taken from their customers. Under a fixed exchange rate regime, the monetary authorities are obliged to supply unlimited quantities of sterling at the current exchange rate. If the exchange rate is fixed, there is the obvious probability that the balance of payments surplus will persist and so will the monetary expansion. In a floating regime, by contrast, with no intervention by the authorities, the price of sterling will rise, with two consequences. Firstly, the quantity of sterling supplied to bank customers in exchange for foreign currency will diminish, thereby reducing the rate of expansion of the sterling money stock. Secondly, the appreciation of the currency will itself reduce and possibly eliminate the balance of payments surplus which was the origin of the problem.

Table 3.6 summarises these possible sources of monetary growth and distinguishes between those which rely upon an initial excess ratio of balances to deposits (using up some of that excess when they occur and thus pushing banks nearer to the limit) and those sources of monetary growth which carry with them a simultaneous and equal increase in bankers' balances and therefore a rise in balances to deposits ratio.

Table 3.6 Sources of monetary growth

Source	Effect on M_s	Effect on excess ratio of balances : deposits
1. Banks lend to the non-bank private sector	+	−
2. Banks purchase securities from the non-bank private sector	+	−
3. Banks purchase goods or services from the non-bank private sector	+	−
4. Government borrowing		
(a) Government sells securities to the Bank of England	+	+
(b) Government sells securities to the banks	+	−
(c) Bank of England lends to the government, selling Treasury bills to the banks	+	+*
5. Balance of payments surplus	+	+

* On the assumption that the Bank of England stands ready to exchange these for balances on demand.

APPENDIX   Financial intermediation and velocity

In Chapter 3 we referred to the fact that recent years had seen a rapid growth in the business of financial intermediaries – firms whose business it is to mediate between savers and borrowers. This they do by creating financial assets (for example, building society deposits or life insurance policies), and selling these assets to the public in return for money which is then on-lent to a variety of borrowers – the personal sector, companies and the government. The intermediaries make a profit essentially on the difference between the interest (or other benefits) paid to the public holding the assets created and the interest charged to the borrowers. The fact that savers and borrowers are prepared to pay middlemen to provide this service rather than to lend and borrow directly between each other at what would, in principle, be a lower cost is usually explained and justified by the fact that the intermediaries are using their skills and experience to create assets and liabilities which match the needs of borrowers and lenders more closely than would otherwise be the case. Taking once again the familiar example of the building societies, it is argued that the huge increase in deposits they have received in the last twenty years indicates their success in creating just the kind of financial asset which the public wanted to hold: highly liquid, interest-bearing and secure. The deposits of money received have been used by the societies to lend to growing numbers of people wishing to buy their own homes. The attraction of the building societies from the borrowers' point of view is that they are prepared to grant a very long-term liability, typically a repayment period of twenty years. If lenders and borrowers had to confront each other directly it is very unlikely that any such volume of lending, borrowing and house purchase could take place. The number of people currently holding their life savings in building society deposits, redeemable on demand, who would be prepared to lend to an unknown house purchaser for a minimum of twenty years must be very few indeed. Considered from the other end, few house purchasers would be willing to buy the family home by borrowing two or three times their current annual salary from a large number of people, any one of whom could ask for repayment on demand. Financial intermediation, by matching the needs of lenders and borrowers, encourages lending and borrowing and therefore some kinds of expenditure which would not otherwise take place.

APPENDIX: FINANCIAL INTERMEDIATION AND VELOCITY

The inclusion of these assets created by intermediaries (**their liabilities**) in liquidity aggregates such as PSL_1 and PSL_2, however, reflects the view that the creation of such assets can influence the level of total spending in an economy. If that is the case then we are saying that the growth of financial intermediation affects the velocity of circulation and that PSL_1 and PSL_2 are measuring simultaneously a mixture of changes in money stock and velocity.

Formally, this is easy to prove. We define the money stock proper as notes and coin in circulation with the non-bank private sector together with bank deposits (of any kind, for the sake of argument). We accept the identity that total current expenditure equals total output at market prices in any period (i.e. $M_s V = PY$) and the definition of V as the number of times the existing money stock has to turnover in order to finance that aggregate expenditure (i.e. $\frac{PY}{M_s} = V$). Now, if PY increases as a result of increased non-bank financial intermediation and there has been no change in the quantity of notes and coin and bank deposits (i.e. $M_s = M_s$), then the only possible result is an increase in V.

For many of us, however, seeing the proof is separable from understanding the process. Let us begin by assuming a fixed stock of notes and coin and bank deposits. This stock of money at the outset must obviously be distributed in some way – that is, the non-bank private sector has shared between its members the physical possession of the notes and coin and the legal ownership of and the right to draw cheques on the bank deposits. Now let us imagine that there emerges for the first time a non-bank financial intermediary in the form of a building society which offers, in exchange for money, an asset which is similar (in liquidity terms) but offers a rate of interest. Some members of the non-bank private sector purchase building society deposits by handing over to the building society an equal quantity of bank deposits. So far, nothing has happened to the size of the money stock. Certainly the building society has not 'created' any money. What has happened, however, is that the ownership of the existing stock has changed. It is still held by the non-bank private sector but some of the bank deposits have changed ownership. They appear in the banks' records now as being the property of the building society. By contrast, there has been an increase in total liquidity. We now have the original money stock **plus** some similar but notably different assets, the building society deposits owned by those who surrendered some bank deposits.

THE SUPPLY OF MONEY

This might be regarded as the first round in the process because it does not, by itself, show any reason why expenditure on real goods and services should change. We have a greater stock of liquid assets but, since we know we cannot buy anything with the extra assets (building society deposits have to be converted into cheques drawn on bank deposits or into notes and coin and the stock of these has not changed), what, we might ask, is all the fuss about?

The next step is to recall that the process of intermediation involves the funds received by the intermediary in exchange for the newly created assets being on-lent to borrowers. In our example, the building society is only temporarily in possession of the bank deposits it received. Fairly quickly, it issues a cheque drawn on part of these deposits to a borrower who is about to purchase a house. Part of the bank deposits once again changes hands. (It would be simpler if we could assume that all building society's bank deposits were transferred to the name of the borrower but, like banks, building societies have to retain some bank deposits to meet those occasions when withdrawals by depositors exceed the inflow of funds.) The borrower uses the transferred bank deposit to buy the house from the current owner who becomes the recipient and new owner of the bank deposit. If he was selling the house to buy another, the process would repeat itself; if he was the builder of a new house, the transferred deposit would be split up before being transferred in constituent parts to employees and suppliers of building materials. The original deposit is being spent and respent.

Summarising the process, we may say that before the intervention of the financial intermediary some part of the money stock was being held as a store of wealth or as idle balances by savers. The achievement of the intermediary was to persuade savers to hold something else (a building society deposit) in its place and to channel the idle money balances to those who wished to use them to buy goods and services. The money stock is unchanged in size but some part of it is now circulating more rapidly than it previously was: total velocity has increased.

We have chosen the example here of a building society, for reasons largely of familiarity but also because their rapid growth, and conspicuous high street presence has captured the public imagination to the point where they are regarded (and used) almost as banks. The principle illustrated by the example, however, is of general applicability in understanding the role of financial intermediation and its effects upon expenditure. If insurance companies accept cash premiums and channel them into corporate investment projects and finance houses accept funds which are subsequently lent to finance consumer spending, the same velocity-increasing process is at work. Indeed, it is worth a note in passing that the building society boom which has received so much attention is geared to channelling funds into a trade in second-hand assets (existing houses) whose purchase does not appear in national output computations and has little employment significance. That some part of building society lending finances the purchase of **new** houses (together with the familiarity of the case) preserves the legitimacy of our example, but if the interest in financial intermediation is its effect upon nominal income, the fact remains that building societies may not be the most relevant case.

QUESTIONS

Essay questions

1. What are the functions of money? What factors determine how much money there is in the British economy at any one time? (JMB)

2. 'Commercial banks cannot simply create money by the liberal use of fountain pens (or computers); they can only make advances or buy assets with cash they have received from depositors and so cannot "create" anything.' Discuss. (WJEC)

3. Outline the major commercial factors which influence the distribution and growth of a commercial bank's assets. In what ways has the Bank of England influenced the structure of bank balance sheets in the UK during the last ten years? (I of B)

4. How do banks create credit? What are the limitations on their power to create credit? (C)

Discussion questions

1. Why can banks manage with such small holdings of liquid reserves?

2. What is the thinking behind such a measure of money as M_2?

3. How does the method of government borrowing determine its impact on the money stock?

4. Why are there so many measures of the money stock?

FURTHER READING

Definitions of the money stock are included in many texts. **The Bank of England Quarterly Bulletin**, December 1982, has still the most detailed analysis. Since the authorities continue to search for new useful definitions, however, continuous updating is necessary. The *BEQB* again can be relied on to report major changes, and the Treasury's *Economic Progress Reports* often have useful articles. Nos 162 and 163 (November, December 1983) discuss, respectively, broad and narrow definitions. Balance sheets of the monetary sector are regularly in *BEQB* and the monthly publication *Financial Statistics* (HMSO) carries some of the same information as well as up-to-date figures for the size of monetary aggregates. *Barclays Review*, LIX, February 1984, also carries a useful article.

A brief but useful summary of the institutions comprising the post-1981 monetary sector is in Brown (1982) and a list of the institutions by name appears in each March issue of *BEQB*. A recent and very readable account of what financial intermediaries do is Wilson (1982), and a more detailed (but strictly pre-1981) survey is in Carter and Partington (1981).

Most texts can be relied upon to explain why an increase in bank lending increases the money stock but few go to the lengths of Section 3.4 here. Llewellyn *et al.* (1982) Ch. 3 covers this ground in a rather theoretical way.

That non-bank financial intermediation increases velocity but not the money stock is also commonly remarked upon, but frequently unexplained. Carter and Partington (Ch. 3) is an exception. Dennis (1981) Ch. 7 is helpful but a little brief. A more step-by-step approach is in Hockley (1970) Ch. 5.

4 METHODS OF MONETARY CONTROL

There are three approaches to monetary control we wish to examine: reserve asset and the related monetary base control; direct controls; interest rate control. The last is the method favoured by the authorities in recent years, replacing the direct controls of an earlier period.

4.1 RESERVE ASSETS AND THE MONETARY BASE

Reserve asset control rests on the assumption that banks maintain a rigid relationship between their deposit liabilities and some form of highly liquid reserve assets. Banks' balances at the Bank of England are an obvious example of the ultimate reserve asset, but in a sophisticated and developed financial system other easily realisable but slightly less liquid assets such as call money and Treasury bills might be included as serving much the same purpose of enabling banks to meet a sudden demand for withdrawals and transfers.

If the banks do maintain a rigid ratio of deposits to reserve assets, and if the authorities can influence the stock of reserve assets (by, for example, the buying and selling of government stock as described earlier), it follows that they can induce a multiple expansion/contraction of deposits. This gives rise to the well-known bank credit multiplier examples and also to the term 'fractional reserve banking' – 'fractional' because reserves are a fraction of deposits. The principle is quite simple. We assume a desired reserve ratio or fraction of 10 per cent. The reserves in question are money at call and bankers' balances. The banks' initial position is set out in Table 4.1. The Bank of England sells

71

METHODS OF MONETARY CONTROL

Table 4.1 Banks' initial position

Liabilities		Assets	
Deposits	1000	Bankers' balances	50
		Money at call	50
		Securities	200
		Loans	700
Total	1000	Total	1000

Ratio of reserves to deposits = 10%

government securities of 50 which are bought by customers of the banks. Their bank deposits are consequently reduced by 50 and the banks, in making payment on their behalf, transfer 50 from their own balances to the account of the government at the Bank of England. Liabilities and assets still balance but there is a prob-

Table 4.2 Banks' interim position

Liabilities		Assets	
Deposits	950	Bankers' balances	0
		Money at call	50
		Securities	200
		Loans	700
Total	950	Total	950

Ratio of reserves to deposits = 5.26%

Table 4.3 Banks' final position

Liabilities		Assets	
Deposits	500	Bankers' balances	25
		Money at call	25
		Securities	100
		Loans	350
Total	500	Total	500

Ratio of reserves to deposits = 10%

lem now regarding the reserve position: liquid reserves are now only 5.26 per cent of deposits.

If the original ratio is to be preserved, deposits must fall to 500. To achieve this the banks sell securities to the public who surrender deposits in payment and they call in some part of their loans. In addition, banks recall some of the money at call in order to restore the original balance between call money and bankers' balances.

A reduction in balances of 50 has led to a tenfold contraction of bank deposits. There has been a contraction of the balance sheet and a rearrangement on the asset side.

Since such a system of monetary control has never been used in the UK there would be little point in pursuing it beyond the barest outline of principle but for two reasons.

The first of these is that references to ratios do appear in banking literature over the years. 'Cash ratios', 'liquidity ratios' and 'reserve asset ratios' have all been specified at times, either by the authorities or by the banks' descriptions of their own prudential practices. The latest of these was the $12\frac{1}{2}$ per cent 'eligible assets' ratio of the 'Competition and Credit Control' era from 1971 to 1981. We have already established that banks **must** maintain some prudential balance between the volume of their deposit business and their ability to meet withdrawal and transfer requests. This tells us nothing about monetary control, however, which requires that the authorities actively seek to manipulate the supply of reserve assets so as to induce multiple expansion/contraction of deposits. This they have never done. Indeed, in the case of the 'eligible assets' ratio of 'Competition and Credit Control' such manipulation would have been impossible since some reserve assets were liabilities of the private sector; their supply was therefore outside the authorities' control and since some of them were held by the non-bank public, banks could always counteract a squeeze by bidding them away from non-bank holders. Even so, the idea has captured the imagination of sufficient observers to produce numerous text book lists of the various assets involved, to the exclusion of any discussion of the way in which controls were in practice operated.

The second reason is that under the pressure of recent events – specifically the poor record of monetary control in the 1970s and the arrival in 1979 of a government even more committed than its predecessors to accurate control of the money supply – proposals have been made for the adoption in future of a

73

system similar to that just described and known as 'monetary base control'. The idea of a 'monetary base' we first encountered in Section 3.1, where we noted the Bank of England's monitoring of the wide monetary base comprising notes and coin and banks' balances at the Bank of England. In a system of monetary base control the base would in practice be narrowed to the stock of banks' balances. Bankers' balances are chosen for control because they are the one asset essential to prudent banking and are the liabilities uniquely of the Bank of England.

In a system of monetary base control, the authorities would announce a target rate of growth for base money of, say, 3 per cent per quarter and buy and sell securities to the non-bank public to enforce that rate of growth. If the banks observe a rigid ratio of deposits to balances, then it follows that the total of deposits will be constrained to grow at the same rate. Deposit growth is constrained in the following manner: If banks find their deposits growing more rapidly than the supply of base money they may try to increase their holdings of the base by selling securities to the public. This cannot increase the amount of base money in the system – if any one bank gains balances it will be at the expense of others – but it will reduce deposits (by the value of security sales) and it will raise interest rates as security prices fall. A rise in interest rates will further help the reduction in deposits by discouraging the demand for loans.

Another possibility is that an individual bank may raise its interest rates to attract depositors from other banks. Once again, however, this will not change the total of base money. Initially it will redistribute the existing stock but, as all banks try to compete deposits from each other, the original distribution is likely to remain much as it was. However, as interest rates have risen, once again, the demand for bank loans will have fallen.

This is the sort of approach that commentators must be presumed to have in mind when drawing the diagram of money market equilibrium shown in Fig. 4.1.

Via the processes described above, reducing the supply of base money would reduce total deposits and the rise in interest rates would induce people to manage with the smaller stock of money.

Sometimes this process is presented in the form of a multiplier. If D stands for bank deposits, R for reserves or bankers' balances, M_s for the money stock and C for notes and coin then, as we saw with the balance sheets earlier, a change in the stock of reserves

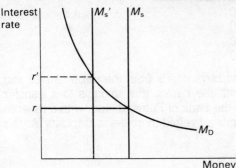

Fig. 4.1

will produce a change in the volume of bank deposits, the size of which depends upon the ratio of reserves to deposits. Formally:

$$\triangle D = \triangle R \cdot \frac{1}{R/D}$$

Therefore, if $M_s = C + D$,

$$\triangle M_s = \triangle C + (\triangle R \cdot \frac{1}{R/D})$$

If notes and coin are themselves treated as part of the reserve base (i.e. in addition to bankers' balances) the principle remains the same but the algebra becomes more complex because we have now to bear in mind that the proportion of currency held by the public determines the proportion available to banks and, therefore, alters the stock of reserves plus currency against which they can create deposits. If C/D represents the public's desired ratio of currency to deposits, then

$$\triangle M_s = \triangle(C + R) : \frac{1 + C/D}{C/D + R/D}$$

By way of illustration, we can imagine a situation where the public's desired ratio of cash to deposits (C/D) is 10 per cent (0.1) and banks' desired ratio of reserves to deposits (R/D) is 20 per cent (0.2). Suppose we are initially in equilibrium with a money stock (M_s) of 1100 composed of notes and coin (C) and bank deposits (D). Because we are in equilibrium, our desired ratios must hold. Therefore, we have

$$M_s = (C + D) = 1100$$
$$C = 100$$
$$D = 1000$$
$$R = 200$$

If the government now buys bonds from the public for 20 and this sum is deposited with the banks, this amounts to a transfer of 20 to their reserves at the Bank of England, and, with a reserve ratio of 20 per cent permits a fivefold increase in deposits. At this interim stage we have

$$M_s = (C + D) = 1200$$
$$C = 100$$
$$D = 1100$$
$$R = 220$$

But this is not an equilibrium position since the public no longer has sufficient cash in relation to deposits. $\frac{100}{1100}$ = 9 per cent while the desired ratio is 10 per cent.) An exchange of deposits for cash takes place. The volume of deposits falls as banks pay out cash to customers but so, crucially, do their balances at the Bank of England as some of these are converted into notes and coin with which to pay customers. This forces some contraction of deposits from the level to which they originally rose until a new level is reached at which the reserve ratio is satisfied, given the public's desire to hold cash. Rounding to one place of decimals, we shall find that the equilibrium solution is

$$M_s = (C + D) = 1173.2$$
$$C = 106.6$$
$$D = 1066.6$$
$$R = 213.4$$
$$M_s = 1173.2 - 1100 = 73.2$$

and we can confirm this result by substituting the illustrative values into the formula:

$$M_s = (20) \cdot \frac{1 + 0.1}{0.1 + 0.2}$$

$$= 20 \cdot \frac{1.1}{0.3}$$

$$= 20 \cdot 3.666$$

$$= 73.2$$

It is a deceptively simple way of controlling the money supply. Since bankers' balances **are** an essential requirement of sound banking, controlling their size **must** constrain the banks' ability to create deposits. Milton Friedman has expressed the view that it is like controlling the output of cars by limiting the available supply of steel – potentially very effective. From the point of view of governments committed to target rates of growth of the money stock it is particularly attractive since the growth rate, once established, cannot be pushed off course by exogenous shocks. If the demand for money shifts as a result of expectations of increased inflation, for example, this will have no effect upon the money stock, only upon the rate of interest necessary to produce equilibrium, as shown in Fig. 4.2.

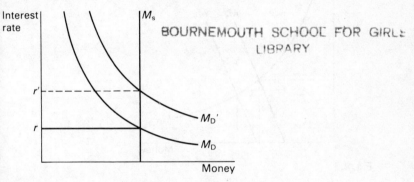

Fig. 4.2

This is an important distinction between monetary base control and the interest rate method of control currently favoured. Under monetary base control, the money stock is the target variable and the rate of interest is the consequence of the target money stock and the strength of money demand.

If the principle is so straightforward and so obviously relevant to governments with money stock targets, it is legitimate to ask why it is not used.

The first difficulty (which our description has conveniently ignored) is that the banks' prudential base requirement is not fixed for all circumstances. There may, in practice, be no ratio of deposits to base money which banks feel always obliged to maintain. Part of the reason for holding reserves is to be prepared for customer withdrawals. Such an eventuality is a risk only with sight deposits, however; where the deposit has been made for a period, as with a time deposit, instant withdrawal is not a risk. Thus, the quantity of balances required will depend not just on the total of deposits but upon the division of those deposits between sight and time. If we add the reasonable supposition that customers will move this distribution towards time deposits as interest rates rise, then, as interest rates rise, a smaller quantity of reserves will be needed. In other words, for a given stock of reserves, as interest rates rise, the greater will be the volume of deposits that can be supported. Taking account of this produces an upward sloping money supply schedule, as in Fig. 4.3.

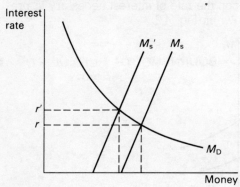

Fig. 4.3

A given change in monetary base produces a smaller change in money stock and interest rates than it would have done under a rigid ratio. The stability of banks' holdings of base money may be revealed by the current Bank of England monitoring programme.

It is sometimes argued that a mandatory requirement would solve this problem of variability. Whatever their own view of prudential requirements, banks would not be able to operate below the mandatory ratio level. Setting a minimum level, however, would still leave the consequences of changes in the base uncertain since, with experience of base control, banks would be free to accumulate reserves above the minimum level in times of 'easy' policy which they could use to thwart the intentions of the authorities when the base were next squeezed.

A second obstacle to the operation of a monetary base system in the UK originates, paradoxically, from one of its attractions. We earlier said that an attraction of base control was that once the stock of reserves was fixed, assuming a constant ratio, the money stock was also fixed. No actions by the banks or their customers, and no changes in the demand for money could affect it. Any unforeseen circumstance would merely result in an adjustment in the rate of interest required to accommodate demand to the fixed supply. It is clear from this that the price to be paid for potentially accurate control of supply (the money stock) will be considerable fluctuation in market price (the rate of interest). Depending on the shape of the demand curve and the length of time period which the authorities were prepared to allow for adjustment, interest rate fluctuations could be very violent indeed. For a number of reasons – the effect on investment, on mortgage holders and on government debt prices – governments in the UK have traditionally been averse to interest rate volatility.

The third and probably largest hurdle facing a system of monetary base control is the fear it inspires of 'disintermediation'. By disintermediation we mean the forcing of business away from recognised UK banks towards other types of financial intermediary at home or abroad. Since financial intermediation still takes place, the term is somewhat misleading: we ought perhaps to think of it as meaning bank-disintermediation. Banks obviously dislike it, since it means they lose business. The authorities are also very wary of it because of what it means to them. Firstly, if would-be bank borrowers manage to borrow from elsewhere, expenditure may still take place, thus thwarting the purpose of the controls. Secondly, this has the effect of distorting the meaning of the official statistics of the money stock which are compiled from returns by banks. The money stock may have been controlled (banks having been forced to restrict lending) but if people manage to borrow from elsewhere and spend, the relationship between the money stock and expenditure is changed (technically, velocity has increased) and the figures no longer mean what they did. This makes both knowing what is happening and controlling it in future very difficult.

Any restriction upon lending which applies only to a specific group of institutions and is intended to limit their lending to less than their customers are willing to pay for, is liable to encourage disintermediation from that group of institutions. We shall encounter it again in the next section as a difficulty which confronted direct controls of banks' lending when they were in use in the 1950s and 1960s. If a system of monetary base control were introduced in present circumstances, many of the same consequences might follow.

Finding a great unsatisfied demand for loans, non-bank financial intermediaries would grow rapidly by offering higher interest rates to attract deposits to lend to dissatisfied bank customers. Banks themselves, might retaliate by encouraging customers to borrow from overseas (uncontrolled) branches. In the absence of exchange controls and **with** highly developed spot and forward markets in foreign exchange, there is only a small cost involved to customers in taking a loan in foreign currency, arranged overseas, and converting it to sterling.

4.2 DIRECT CONTROLS

Direct controls of a variety of kinds have been used over the years to control the growth of bank deposits. In the 1950s and 1960s the controls consisted of 'lending ceilings' and 'qualitative guidance'. For reasons we shall see shortly, disenchantment led to Edward Heath's government turning from direct controls to the 'market based' approach of Competition and Credit Control in 1971. In spite of this, calls for 'supplementary special deposits' which occurred in the 1970s, because of the way they penalised banks that exceeded lending targets, could also be regarded as a form of direct control.

Lending ceilings, or quantitative guidance, were instructions to banks to restrict the growth of their lending to some predetermined official target rate. In extreme cases this might be zero, but was more usually a positive figure set below the rate which might otherwise have been expected in the light of the experience of immediately preceding years. Instructions on the quantity of lending might also be accompanied by 'qualitative guidance' – that is, guidance on the composition of lending. Usually, such guidance would be to favour exporters and industrial investment and to discourage personal borrowing and borrowing for property dealing. Although most commonly used alongside quantitative advice, such qualitative guidance could itself, if sufficiently tightly drawn, have quantitative implications.

In the 1950s and 1960s such guidance worked without overt threat to banks in the event of non-compliance (hence, occasional reference to it as 'moral-suasion'). No doubt, though, part of the reason for their co-operation was the knowledge that the Bank, if necessary, could seek coercive powers from the government. Direct controls give several advantages. Firstly, they are effective in controlling the growth of the money supply, because, as we have seen, banks have always complied with the instructions. Also, they can be introduced at short notice and be made to discriminate between different types of borrower. Probably their greatest attraction from the authorities' point of view, however, is that direct controls can be used to curb monetary growth without having to resort to higher interest rates. Whatever the demand for bank lending, banks would supply only the quantity permitted under the current regulations. This meant that banks had to devise and operate some form of non-price rationing of loans, favouring customers of long standing or with large accounts, always provided that such customers met the qualifications which might be part of the official guidelines.

The fact that direct controls require some form of non-price rationing, however, meant that banks were engaged in a volume of lending which, had it been undertaken at the market-clearing level of interest rates, would have been much more profitable to them; for this reason alone it would have been unwelcome. It also created two related difficulties which have encouraged the monetary authorities in recent years to rely more upon 'market based' methods.

The first of these was that the banks themselves resented the discrimination they had to perform between customers who, on a purely commercial basis, were all eligible for bank finance. They found it understandably invidious to have to turn away clients with proposals which both parties could see were commercially sound on the grounds that the client was in the wrong, or at least less favoured, line of business, while other customers were receiving help for schemes which commercially were no better. There was also a suspicion, on the part of banks, that their persistent refusal of finance to sound customers would lead to the latter taking their business to rival, non-bank, financial institutions. Economists objected to such controls on the standard theoretical ground that non-price discrimination leads to a misallocation of resources. In particular, there were fears that large firms, being important customers, were likely to get the limited bank finance systematically at the expense of smaller firms which might, however, be very important for enterprise and future growth.

The second difficulty was that of 'disintermediation'. In the light of experience, banks were right to fear that persistently turning away customers who were prepared to pay for what they wanted would encourage the supply of finance from other quarters. Since banks alone were normally the subject of control, there was nothing to prevent disappointed borrowers turning to insurance companies, finance houses and other, non-bank, financial intermediaries for help. To economists, this seems utterly predictable and not necessarily a bad thing, but to the authorities it was unwelcome for three reasons. Firstly, it meant that direct controls – although effective in discouraging the growth of bank deposits and, therefore, of the measured money stock – were less effective in controlling expenditure. This could still increase by making more intensive use of the existing money stock. Technically, borrowing from non-banks was increasing the velocity of circulation in the way we described in the appendix to Chapter 3. Secondly, the diversion of bank business to other institutions meant that if controls were to be effective in future, they would have to be spread over a much wider range of institutions. In an attempt to protect themselves from this diversion of their business, banks developed interests in forms of non-bank financial intermediation by establishing legally independent companies to which the regulations did not apply. Thirdly, and perhaps uppermost in the minds of the authorities, was the fact that disintermediation distorted the meaning of the official monetary statistics. It is bank deposits which appear in measures of the money stock. If the method of monetary control limits the growth of both only by forcing borrowing into 'unofficial' channels, then not only is monetary control failing in its ultimate objective to control spending, but it is also making it very difficult for the authorities to know what the true position is. A good example is provided by the abolition of 'the corset' or supplementary special deposit scheme which had placed a quantitative limit on the growth of bank deposits in certain years of the 1970s. During the periods of constraint, firms switched their borrowing to non-banks or issued their own commercial bills. These were then 'accepted' or guaranteed by banks and sold by firms to the non-bank public. The spending of firms, therefore, continued pretty much as it would have done had they borrowed from banks and the public's liquidity position had scarcely changed by surrendering cash for a very close substitute, the bank-guaranteed bill. When the corset was abolished in June 1980 this 'bill-leak' was estimated to be nearly £3 bn. After abolition, as borrowing switched back to more conventional bank channels, it was recorded as an addition to the money stock, producing a sudden upsurge in the official figures.

4.3 INTEREST RATE CONTROL

In the next section of this chapter we shall be discussing the operation of monetary control since 1981 in some detail. Central as it is to current methods of control, only sufficient outline is required here to permit a contrast to be drawn with the methods so far discussed.

At the heart of interest rate control lies the belief that the demand for bank loans by the public is inversely related to the rate of interest payable on these loans. Thus, if the authorities can engineer a rise in interest rates, the demand for loans will fall and so too will the pace at which banks can create deposits.

In practice, the Bank of England seeks to influence interest rates by its operations in the discount market. If banks find themselves short of balances at the Bank of England we know that their first line of reserve liquidity is money placed at call with discount houses who have used it to purchase Treasury and commercial bills. The banks' demanding repayment of call money from the discount houses passes the liquidity problem to the latter who look to the Bank of England for help either in the form of a loan or as a purchaser for cash of some of the houses' holdings of bills. By longstanding agreement, the Bank is always ready to do this but can choose the rate of interest (charged on the loan) or the rate of discount (at which it buys the bills). Providing relief at a rate of interest/discount above that currently prevailing in the market is a signal that the Bank wishes to see rates rise and many institutions will follow the lead as a matter of convention. Even if they did not, however, market forces would ensure eventual compliance.

The shortage of banks' cash balances which began this sequence of events can come about either as the result of normal market trading or as a result of deliberate action by the Bank. In the normal course of events, each day will see considerable transfers between clients of the banks and the government. As we noted earlier, a net transfer towards the government will reduce banks' cash balances and therefore the ratio of balances to deposits. Failing this result of normal trading, the Bank can always create the net transfer by sales of government debt to the non-bank public.

There are obviously a number of potential difficulties with such an approach. Firstly, it is aimed largely at controlling private sector bank deposits. The public sector's demand for bank credit is unlikely to be very interest-sensitive, being determined largely by the level of its expenditure and what it can raise in revenue from taxation and borrowing from the non-bank public. Relying on interest rates to control monetary growth, therefore, assumes that 'appropriate' policies regarding the level of expenditure, taxation and sales of debt to the non-bank public are being pursued by the public sector.

Interest rate control also relies heavily on a stable and interest-sensitive demand for bank credit by the private sector. Obviously if the demand is insensitive (as in Fig. 4.4) a larger variation in interest rates will be required in order to produce a reduction in the demand for and supply of bank loans than would be the case if it were interest-sensitive (as in Fig. 4.5).

If the demand is also unstable in relation to interest rates, the position of the curve will shift and the demand for and supply of bank credit associated with any given level of interest rates becomes uncertain: in Fig. 4.6 a rise in interest rates from r_1 to r_2 is accompanied by an increase in bank lending because demand coincidentally has increased for non-interest rate reasons.

4.4 MONETARY CONTROL SINCE 1981

Since 1976, in fact, the target of monetary control has been the annual rate of growth of the money stock, defined as $£M_3$. The Conservative government, since taking office in 1979, has modified the practice by publishing target rates of growth for up to five years ahead, together with projections for other, related, magnitudes such as the Public Sector Borrowing Requirement (PSBR). Achieving mutually consistent growth paths for these magnitudes is the object of the Medium-Term Financial Strategy (MTFS). Since 1982, the MTFS has included target rates of growth additionally for M_1 and PSL_2.

As the following statement by the Governor of the Bank of

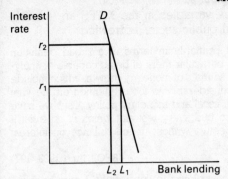

Fig. 4.4

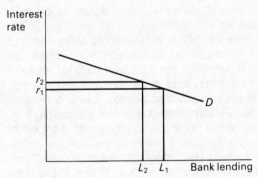

Fig. 4.5

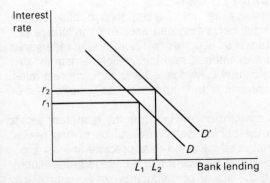

Fig. 4.6

85

England illustrates, the key variables in the MTFS are interest rates, the money stock and public sector borrowing.

. . .We have always thought primarily in terms of a broad definition of money . . . it [£M$_3$] has the particular merit of being capable of analysis in terms of the counterpart sources of monetary growth, which include the PSBR. This has helped considerably to focus attention on the vital need for consistency between fiscal and monetary policy. Thus we have attached particular attention to budgetary restraint which is essential if monetary control is to be effective without undue reliance on interest rates.

(**BEQB** June 1983, 197)

In this section we want to explain the connection between public sector borrowing, monetary growth and interest rates and hence the need for 'monetary and fiscal consistency'. We shall also look at the most recent changes in the Bank's methods of influencing these variables.

Recalling the definition of £M$_3$ as consisting of notes and coin in circulation and private sector bank deposits, we can see that what happens to £M$_3$ depends for the most part on what happens to the community's total borrowing from the monetary sector. Deposits will increase (as explained in Section 3.4) as a result of net new bank lending. Clearly, changes in the community's indebtedness to the banks can originate with borrowing by either the public or the private sectors. It makes no significant difference that the public sector's bank deposits are no longer themselves included in £M$_3$ (as they were prior to March 1984). If the public sector borrows from the banking system, the borrowed funds will appear as an increase in the money stock the moment they are received by the private sector.

The authorities employ one set of techniques to influence the growth of public sector borrowing and another to influence private sector borrowing. It so happens that both sets of techniques have, fortunately, similar interest rate implications – namely, that slow growth or tight control is associated with high interest rates. We begin by examining the approach to public sector borrowing.

Changes in public sector borrowing from the monetary sector occur as a result of the public sector's overall borrowing needs. This elementary point is all we need to appreciate at least a potential connection between the PSBR and a change in the money stock. Unfortunately, the actual connection is not so simple that we can say that the PSBR is **equivalent to** a change in the money stock. Given, for example, a PSBR of £5 bn., some part of the required total may be obtained by borrowing from members of the public (by selling government stock or encouraging the take-up of national savings facilities). In this case, there is merely a transfer of **existing** bank deposits from members of the public to the government. There is no change in the total of bank deposits and no change in the money stock. Thus, we must modify our original statement and say that the change in public sector borrowing which is relevant to a change in total bank deposits depends on **both** the size of the PSBR and the way in which it is financed. There will be a change in public sector deposits affecting the total volume of deposits if there is an increase in public sector borrowing and no corresponding reduction in other bank deposits. This will come about if the public sector borrows from the banking system because, in these circumstances, bank deposits (liabilities) are being **created** against the assets (government stock or whatever) which are offered to the banks in exchange. Banks will have created new liabilities and therefore new money. It may be some comfort to recall that this is only restating a process we earlier encountered in Section 3.4.

Putting this back into the context of the PSBR, this amounts to saying that the impact upon the money stock (the change in bank lending to the UK public sector) will be equal to the PSBR **minus** all other forms of public sector borrowing. Thus, we may summarise: the increase in sterling bank lending to the public sector equals

the PSBR   **minus** public sector borrowing from overseas and in foreign currency

                 minus the sale of debt to the non-bank public

                 minus the increase in cash held by the non-bank public.

This may seem a very cumbersome way of arriving at the rather obvious conclusion that there will be an increase in the money stock if the public sector borrows from the banks just as there would be if members of the general public were to do so. However, this little bit of arithmetic draws our attention to two very important points in connection with monetary control. The first is that the overall conduct of fiscal policy has monetary implications (the Governor's 'need for consistency between fiscal and monetary policy'). Fiscal policy refers to the decisions made by governments about revenue (from taxation, charges etc.) and expenditure. These decisions will have a large bearing upon (though they do not alone completely determine) the size of the PSBR with which our arithmetic begins.

What this form of presentation also reveals is the importance of non-bank borrowing to changes in the money stock brought about by the behaviour of public sector deposits. It is only that part of the PSBR financed by borrowing from the banking system that affects the overall size of the money stock. Thus, a large PSBR by itself indicates nothing about the likely behaviour of the money stock. If that borrowing requirement is financed entirely by selling debt to the non-bank public, for example, there will be no effect on the size of the money stock.

So far then we can say that controlling the money stock by controlling the public sector contribution to total bank deposits involves close attention to fiscal policy (to influence the total PSBR) and to debt sales, meaning borrowing from the non-bank public, to determine the proportion of the PSBR which is financed by 'residual' or 'monetary' means.

If we take 'close attention to debt sales' to mean allowing interest rates on government stock and national savings to move to the level necessary to sell the target quantity of debt, then we can see that we are interested in three interrelated variables: the level of interest rates, the size of the PSBR and the rate of monetary growth. The authorities would ideally like to choose values for all three but because of the interrelationships, once values for two have been chosen, it follows that the third has to be accepted. A schematic presentation may help:

For a given . . .	the authorities have to accept . . .
(1) PSBR and $\dot{M}_s$ target	the level of interest rates necessary to sell enough debt to the non-bank private sector to keep residual finance within $\dot{M}_s$ target
(2) PSBR and desired level of r	the quantity of debt the non-bank private sector is willing to buy at that level of r and consequently the amount of residual financing and $\dot{M}_s$
(3) desired level of r and $\dot{M}_s$ target	the conduct of fiscal policy necessary to get the PSBR to a level at which the target level of r leaves a residual financing need consistent with target $\dot{M}_s$

Key:

PSBR = Public Sector Borrowing Requirement

r = interest rate

$\dot{M}_s$ = rate of growth of money stock

Since 1981, the government's conduct of monetary control has most closely approximated the third of these cases. The object of policy has been to fund the government's borrowing needs at the lowest possible level of interest rates consistent with given target rates of growth for £M_3. Low interest rates are desired as a stimulus to private sector investment and slow monetary growth to limit inflation. Given what we have said above, small values for these are attainable only if the PSBR is itself small, and this is the reason for the great deal of attention being given to fiscal policy by a government which has always argued for the importance of monetary policy in maintaining a stable economic environment. The fiscal policy required for a small PSBR could involve either of two possibilities: a high level of public expenditure nearly matched by high tax revenue or a low level of public expenditure with a correspondingly low level of tax revenue. For the present government, a mixture of free market ideology, and a notion that high taxation diminishes incentives has ruled out the first of these combinations, and so we are left with the currently familiar picture of the Treasury struggling to reduce public expenditure to a level which will be more nearly covered by tax revenue and, consequently, leave a smaller PSBR.

The fact that a struggle is involved is the consequence of recession. As unemployment rises, tax revenue falls and public expenditure (because of welfare payments) tends to increase. Both of these raise the level of PSBR above what it would otherwise be. This process is familiar to economists of a Keynesian persuasion. In the standard Keynesian view, reductions in public expenditure without at least equally large reductions in tax revenue work through the multiplier to reduce income and employment. For this reason, Keynesian critics of current policy would argue that it is likely to be self-defeating, more especially if the cuts in public expenditure are of a kind (aid to industry is an example) that will force industry to borrow more from the banks. They would argue that if chasing a small PSBR during a recession appears to have **any** effect on monetary growth it is because the rise in unemployment/fall in output causes a reduction in the demand for active balances.

89

METHODS OF MONETARY CONTROL

The need to finance the existing PSBR by non-monetary means, and to do so at lowest possible interest rates, has led to more adventurous techniques of debt marketing. Recent years have seen the introduction of index-linked, variable rate and part-paid government stocks as well as index-linked and more aggressively marketed national savings instruments. In 1982–83 the borrowing requirement was £9 bn. The success of recent debt management strategy can be seen from the fact that some £10.4 bn. was raised from the domestic non-bank private sector and a further £2 bn. from the external sector. The result was an 'over-funding' of public sector borrowing which allowed the repayment of previous bank borrowing equal to approximately £3 bn. The public sector contribution to monetary growth in 1982–83 was therefore negative.

The control of private sector deposits is based upon the belief that the supply, and therefore the size, of these deposits is demand-determined. This amounts to accepting that whatever quantity of bank borrowing the non-bank private sector wishes to undertake will be met by the banking system. Basic to the system of control as this proposition may be, it also seems strange. It reads like a capitulation, as though the authorities were giving up all hope of control at a time when governments have been moving closer and closer to the view that **strict** monetary control is essential to the economy.

What must be remembered, however, is that the only way to avoid a 'demand-determined' money supply is by limiting the size of the banks' balance sheets. If the authorities do not seek to control the lending policies of banks, then the major components of the demand for loans and the supply of money are simply two sides of those balance sheets. Banks will determine how much they are willing to lend and to whom and competition for deposits and for loans will determine interest rates.

We have already seen that one of the two ways of controlling the size of the banks' balance sheets, direct controls, led in the 1950s and 1960s to disintermediation, thereby extending the area over which control would have had to be exercised and distorting the meaning of official statistics. The alternative, monetary base control, has never been tried (possible reasons appeared in Section 4.1.), though there seems no reason why it also would not lead to disintermediation.

To accept that supply is demand-determined is not the passive position it appears to be if it is possible to influence demand. The demand for bank deposits and in particular for the bank lending which leads to changes in the stock of deposits, is believed to be inversely, and sensitively, related to the rate of interest charged on that lending.

These are not new ideas in the field of monetary control. The view that the best way to influence the growth of private sector bank deposits was to influence demand for loans via interest rates was the foundation of the 'Competition and Credit Control' arrangements introduced in 1971, though, as we noted in Section 4.1 this was obscured for some commentators by the inclusion in these arrangements of a ratio of eligible assets to liabilities. In the words of the then Governor:

> It is not to be expected that the mechanism of a minimum reserve asset ratio and special deposits can be used to achieve some precise multiple contraction or expansion of bank assets. Rather the intention is to use our control over liquidity, which these instruments will reinforce, to influence the structure of interest rates. The resulting change in relative rates of return will induce portfolio shifts . . .
>
> Bank of England, **Competition and Credit Control** (1971) p.8

If we assume a given level of nominal income, a simple diagram will suffice to show the relationship between interest rates and the demand for bank loans and, therefore, bank deposits. Thus, in Fig. 4.7 at interest rate r_1 the demand for (and the supply of) bank lending will be at B_1 and at r_2 the demand (and the supply) will be B_2.

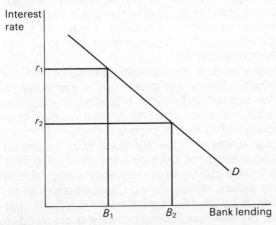

Fig. 4.7

In one respect this is very familiar. A reduction in the supply of bank deposits (and money stock) will be associated with a rise in interest rates. For this reason it is worth pausing to emphasise the difference between what is being described here and the frequently encountered macroeconomic textbook representation of money market equilibrium. That, too, involves an association of high interest rates with 'tight' money. In Fig. 4.8 the money stock is exogenously determined (apparently with great precision) by some process which is not usually explained but which, as we said in Section 4.1, we can assume to be some variant of the reserve asset/fractional reserve/monetary base kind. Whatever it is, in the diagram the money stock is determined exogenously, and **independently of the rate of interest.**

With the money stock fixed at M_s, equilibrium will prevail at interest rate r_1. That is to say, the money stock M_s will be willingly held by the community because individual attempts to hold some different quantity of money, by exchanging money balances with financial assets, has pushed the yield on those assets to the point where the cost of holding the officially determined money stock makes it just worthwhile. If the money stock is reduced to M_s', the immediate result at the existing rate of interest is to leave people short of the money balances they would wish to hold at that price. The individual response is to sell financial assets for money to replenish those balances. This, of course, cannot change the aggregate money stock which has been reduced by official action. The sale of assets merely redistributes the holdings of the reduced money stock (and of the assets) but, more crucially, it depresses the price of the assets, raising the yield, as in Fig. 4.9 to the level at which it seems worth managing with reduced money balances after all.

In short, the money stock is exogenously determined and, for a given money demand, the rate of interest is the **consequence** of the interaction of demand and supply. It is worth pushing this illustration just one stage further in the light of what we shall have to say about difficulties of monetary control in Section 4.5. Suppose, with the original money stock M_s, there is an increased demand for transaction balances, perhaps because of inflation or because of a rise in real output. Again, by assumption, nothing can happen to the money stock, but individual attempts to increase money holdings by the sale of assets leads to a fall in their price and a rise in the yield until the community is prepared to manage with the existing money stock.

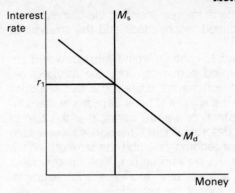

Fig. 4.8

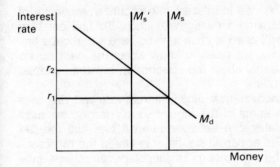

Fig. 4.9

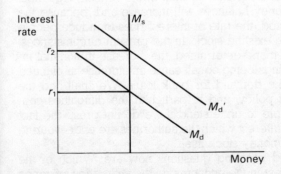

Fig. 4.10

Once again, it is the rate of interest which is the consequence of an exogenously determined money stock and the strength of demand for it.

Now we are in a position to contrast what Galbraith would undoubtedly call this 'accepted sequence' with the 'revised sequence' which we said describes the current conduct of policy (with particular regard to the supply of bank deposits to the non-bank private sector). In practice, we are saying it is the rate of interest which is officially determined and the money stock which is the consequence of that lending rate and the strength of the demand for bank lending. As we said earlier, high interest rates are still associated with 'tight' money. In Fig. 4.7, for example, to obtain a reduction in the supply, the authorities must act to raise interest rates (from r_1 to r_2) to reduce the quantity of loans demanded.

In our version, the rise in interest rate occurs irrespective of the slope of the demand for money function. To find out how much interest rate will need to change to achieve a particular target for money supply, we need to know about the demand for bank loans – in essence, about the relationship between interest rate and spending plans.

In Fig. 4.9, to discover how much interest rate will rise as a result of the achievement of the money supply target, we must know about the relationship between interest rate and the demand for money. The apparent similarity between the two cases is misleading and the implications for monetary control are quite fundamental.

Consider the contrasting circumstances in each case when there is an increase in nominal income. In the familiar sequence, the demand for money balances will increase and, because the money supply is fixed, the rate of interest rises to induce people to manage with the existing stock. In the present circumstances, where supply is demand-determined, the increase in nominal income will, other things being equal, cause an increase in planned expenditure and the demand for bank loans. We shall find the current conduct of policy, and in particular the difficulties confronting it, impossible to understand if we do not grasp the fact that it is the rate of interest which the authorities are endeavouring to set and not the money stock itself.

The obvious and pressing questions now are 'Which of the many rates of interest in the economy do the authorities influence for purposes of monetary control?' and 'How is that influence brought to bear?' The first of these is the more easily answered. The relevant interest rates are those payable on very short-term loans and on financial assets with a very short period to maturity. By 'short' we here mean up to approximately one month. We need to remember that it is the demand for bank loans that the authorities are trying to influence and this is likely to be most strongly influenced by the rate of return on alternative assets which are reasonably close substitutes – that is to say, are highly liquid.

The way in which the authorities seek this influence is less easily described. In particular, answering this question brings us up against certain detailed changes in operating practice which were made in 1981 and which are sometimes said to have made the conduct of policy more 'market-based'. These will be examined shortly, but the most useful start to the description involves a few fundamentals, some of which we touched on in section 3.3 and 3.4, and which are quite unaffected by recent developments.

The starting point has to be the fact that the Bank of England is ultimately, or in a well-known phrase 'the lender of last resort', the sole supplier of liquidity to the monetary system. Remember, the government banks with the Bank of England and if, for whatever reason, there is a net flow of payments from the non-bank private sector to the government, banks as a whole will experience a rundown of their balances at the Bank of England and a reduction in their ratio of 'cash' to deposit liabilities. The only way in which such a shortage can be relieved is by the Bank lending directly to the monetary sector or by buying assets for cash from the monetary sector or the non-bank private sector (who then make deposits of cash with the banks). Remember, too, that in the UK system there has never been any question about such relief always being forthcoming (as there would be under a system of monetary base control). A question does arise (and this is the key) over the terms – principally the rate of interest – on which this help will be forthcoming. The Bank, being a monopoly supplier, can choose the price. If assistance is being supplied, but at a rate of interest higher than that which currently prevails in the market, financial institutions will have to raise the rate of interest charged to customers in order to protect their profits.

This, as a statement of the principles involved, is all we need. The picture becomes more complex, however, once we start to ask questions about the way in which the principles are put into practice. In particular, we need to know through what channels the assistance is provided: which institutions are principally involved? How is the assistance made available at a particular rate of interest? Does the Bank simply lend at a prepublished rate or does it supply funds in exchange for other assets? What happens if the Bank wishes to see interest rates rise (or fall) when there is no shortage (or surplus) of funds in the market? It is answers to questions like these which have been affected by recent changes in operating practice.

The channel through which assistance is given is the discount market; that is to say, the Bank deals directly only with the discount houses. In Section 3.3 we established that the discount houses hold Treasury and commercial bills as assets, having borrowed funds (their liabilities) 'at call' or very short notice from banks in order to make the purchases. Since the funds can be readily recalled by the banks, this makes existing loans to the discount houses the banks' next line of liquidity after the balances held at the Bank of England. Thus, in the event of a shortage of balances, banks will recall existing discount market loans in order to replenish those balances. For the banks, this means a reorganisation on the asset side of the balance sheet. For the discount houses, however, repaying money at call means either the disposal of some earning assets, selling Treasury and commercial bills, or borrowing from some other source to maintain the size of their balance sheet. In the past, assistance frequently took the form of borrowing from the Bank of England, a process known sometimes as 'discount window lending'. The rate of interest to be charged on this lending was published in advance by the Bank, until 1972 known as Bank Rate and until 1981 as Minimum Lending Rate. If such a rate were raised above prevailing market rates, this would be a signal that the Bank wished to see short-term interest rates rise and institutions would generally comply as a matter of convention. Similarly, an unchanged or a falling rate would be interpreted as a general instruction.

Since 1981, however, the Bank has preferred to provide assistance by buying bills from the discount houses rather than by lending at an announced rate. No overt statement is made about the price at which the Bank will buy bills in order to help the houses. Consequently, the **houses** have to formulate their own offer prices for bills. We need to remember that the price at which these bills are bought and sold, represents a discount on their maturity value and therefore in effect a rate of interest. Thus, if the discount houses are severely short of funds, they are likely to compete fairly vigorously among themselves, offering bills to the Bank at a substantial discount, thus establishing a higher discount (rate of interest) than previously existed on these bills. The Bank, for its part, can influence the rate by its response to the offers, turning them all down if, for example, it wished to see interest rates go higher than the houses' initial formulations. The discount houses would then have to make offers at a larger discount. In the final extreme, even under the 1981 arrangements, the Bank has the option of suspending this practice and returning to lending at a pre-announced rate.

When the Bank increases the discount at which it buys bills from the houses, the latter are faced with at worst a loss and at best a reduction in the profit they expected to make when they bought the bills. Minimising this loss has two consequences which help to spread the effect of this rise in interest rates more widely through the system. Firstly, the houses will be prepared to buy bills in future only at a larger discount than would previously have been the case and, because they are the market makers in bills, this will lower the market price of bills generally, increasing their yield and encouraging institutions to hold a greater quantity of bills. Since bills are substitutes for a number of short-term financial assets, a diversion of funds from the latter towards bills will have the effect of raising interest rates on these other assets, and for some institutions the alternative assets may be loans and advances for the non-bank private sector. Secondly, to minimise the loss involved in selling bills to the Bank at an unexpectedly large discount, the houses will be willing to raise the rate paid on borrowed funds from other sources. Among these will be banks for whom 'money at call' has now become more profitable in relation to other assets in their portfolios. In the words of the Bank, this 'change in relative rates of return will induce portfolio shifts . . .' in this case towards money lent at call and away from advances. This reduction in supply, in turn, will raise the rate charged on advances to borrowers who, if the authorities' expectations are confirmed, will borrow less and deposits will increase more slowly.

It is this provision of assistance by the purchase of bills at prices which the houses must formulate which has partly encouraged the view that control is now more 'market-based'. This is true insofar as the price/discount/rate of interest originates with the houses and presumably represents the degree of shortage·in the market. Certainly, market conditions enter the picture here in a way they did not when the Bank announced its own price. On the other hand, it has to be remembered that if the cash shortage is general, then the Bank becomes the monopoly supplier to the houses and can and has used that position to influence the rate of discount/interest. Also, since the rate at which the Bank has actually dealt each day (and the number of bills bought) is published daily, it is unlikely that the houses are going to offer bills at rates of discount significantly different from those at which the Bank has been known to be operating and any trend, upward or downward, can be easily complied with. Lastly, the 'competition' among the sellers of bills must not be exaggerated. There are just ten discount houses, and their everyday business involves frequent contact.

At least as important as this change in dealing practices in 1981 were two other announcements. The first was that the supply of bills in which the Bank could conduct its operations would be increased by widening the range of institutions whose 'acceptances' of the bills would make them eligible. Also, in order to ensure that the houses had sufficient funds with which to trade in bills, banks would be required to hold funds equal to a minimum of 4 per cent and a daily average over six or twelve months of 6 per cent of their liabilities with the discount market. From the point of view of monetary control, the significance of these moves was to enlarge the discount market and to force banks to participate in it at a level which would ensure that the Bank's operations in this market would be bound to have some impact upon them. In recent years, the growth of bank lending between banks (the 'interbank' market) and to the Eurocurrency market, both forms of lending at very short notice, has given banks a source of liquidity outside of the discount or traditional money market. If banks can restore their liquidity position by recalling loans from markets in which the Bank of England has relatively little influence, then the latter's control is potentially diminished. The 1981 measures help to maintain the importance of the traditional money market and therefore the Bank's control.

So far, we have discussed the Bank's efforts to influence short-term interest rates on the assumption that the desired movement is upwards. In the contemporary context, where the emphasis of policy has been generally upon constraining monetary growth within a target range and where success has been very limited, this emphasis is utterly reasonable. By consistently accepting the highest offer price (the smallest discount) the Bank can encourage a fall in interest rates. In the extreme case, where the banks have such a surplus of liquidity that they reduce the interest rate on, and increase the volume of lending to, the discount houses the latter will wish to buy bills from the Bank. If the Bank wishes to see interest rates generally fall, it will supply such bills at a very small discount on their maturity value.

We can formalise both the 'tight' and 'easy' money cases diagrammatically.

Fig. 4.11 shows a period of tight money in which the supply of bills from the discount houses is shown by $S_B{}^0$, with fewer bills being offered for sale, the larger the discount rates. The Bank then chooses the interest rate it requires (r_1) and tailors its acceptance of bills to achieve this rate. As we said above, this may in practice occur over time with offers being submitted and resubmitted after rejection or partial acceptance. If the Bank wishes to raise interest rates, it will choose to reject a higher proportion of offers, forcing the discount houses to resubmit. This is equivalent to moving the exogenous demand for bills curve to the right to D_B1.

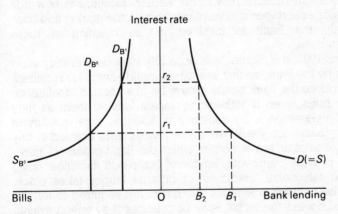

Fig. 4.11

In the easy money case where discount houses seek to reduce their money holdings by buying bills, the position is reversed. Now, 4.12, there is a net demand for bills from the discount houses, indicated by D_B0. The Bank tailors its willingness to sell on the basis of its desired interest rate.

Nowadays, whether the Bank is acting as a buyer or seller in

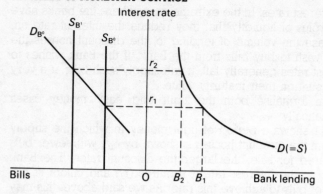

Fig. 4.12

the market, it frequently seems as if it is passively following market trends. The reality is that it is deciding on its supply of or demand for bills so as to produce the interest rate it desires, given its estimate of the strength and direction of other market forces. All that remains now of our earlier questions is how it is that liquidity shortages and surpluses arise in the market and how, if at all, the Bank is involved in the creation of these circumstances.

Before 1981, the market was generally kept deliberately short of funds by the Bank, so that assistance would always be required, and therefore the Bank would always be in a position to influence interest rates, even if 'influencing' meant leaving them as they were. This was done by selling a sufficiently large quantity of Treasury bills each week, which the houses were obliged to buy as their side of an agreement in which the Bank promised, in return, to provide them with 'lender of last resort' facilities. Since 1981 the intentional 'overissue' of bills no longer takes place. Under the new arrangements, the banks are required to tell the Bank of England the target level of balances they intend to hold (and to notify any change in that target level). We know that in the normal course of events each day will see a transfer of funds between the banks and the government which will affect the level of these balances. Using the level of balances it knows the banks wish to hold, and its own forecast of the net daily flow of funds between the public sector and the banks, the Bank of England now forecasts the daily shortage/surplus which is likely to occur and takes steps solely to offset that shortage/surplus. In practice, the estimate, which is announced in the morning, is frequently followed by a midday revision. If the estimate is of a shortage, the Bank announces that it is willing to buy bills and the discount houses are invited to submit offers to which the Bank will respond, in the way already described, depending upon its view of the appropriate level of interest rates. If the estimate is of a surplus, the Bank will invite bids for Treasury bills.

This change in the manner of supplying Treasury bills is another reason for saying that the Bank's operations have become more market-based. This is obviously so in that the Bank is deciding its action in the light of market conditions rather than acting by rule and then taking steps to bring the consequences into line with what the market will bear. It has to be remembered, however, that the 'market conditions' here referred to are determined largely by the flow of funds between the government and the banking system. Insofar as the authorities can influence the magnitude of these flows, then the market conditions are themselves partly the result of official action.

The simplest illustration is provided by the sale of government debt to the non-bank private sector. We have already seen that the sale of debt is one source of a transfer of funds from the banking system to the government. Sufficiently large and sufficiently frequent sales of debt can ensure that the market is always short of funds. For this reason, as we noted at the beginning of this section, controlling the growth of public and private sector deposits is bound to overlap. Large sales of government debt intended to finance public expenditure by non-monetary means will raise longer term interest rates. At the same time, they will produce a shortage of liquidity which helps the Bank to raise short-term interest rates.

We can now pull together and illustrate these various aspects of operating practice by looking at Fig. 4.13, a report of the Bank's dealings on Friday, 23 September 1983, as reported in the **Financial Times** the following day.

The points of interest are the Bank's initial estimate of a shortage of 'around £350 m.'. There is no mention of subsequent revision, though by the end of trading 'total help amounted to £391 m.'. The rest of the report gives a rough indication of the arithmetic. Contributing to the shortage was the maturing of earlier assistance – help given at an earlier date which was now having to be repaid – a sale of Treasury bills to help finance next week's public sector spending requirements (£393 m.) and

101

a rise in the issue of currency notes paid for by the banks by running down their balances (£220 m.). Very little assistance was given in the morning. The Bank purchased a mere £8 m. of bills in maturity band 2 (these mature within 15–33 days and the incident is a reminder that the Bank is trying to restrict its influence to very short-term interest rates). In the afternoon there was a further purchase of £65 m. and, the major source of help, a purchase of £293 m. on the condition that the discount houses agree to buy these back again on 30 September. There was further unspecified assistance of £25 m. later in the day, making the total of £391 m. The rate of discount imposed by the Bank varied between $9\frac{1}{2}$ and $9\frac{3}{4}$ per cent, representing no change on previous days. From the opening lines of the report, it appears that some offers of bills were made with a smaller discount, the houses perhaps sensing the possibility of a reduction in dealing rates, but these were unsuccessful. A glance at the 'Treasury Bills' column of the table tends to confirm this. The rate on bills of two and three months maturity in which the Bank was not dealing suggests the market expected a fall in rates to around 9 per cent within three months.

4.5 PROBLEMS OF MONETARY CONTROL

A system of monetary control which relies upon being able to influence the demand for bank loans via short-term interest rates places great faith in both the interest sensitivity and the stability of the demand for loans. If either condition fails to apply, accurate control will be difficult: the worst case occurs where the demand for loans is both interest-insensitive and unstable. In Fig. 4.14, which approximates the worst case, a slight movement to the right by the demand for loans curve (the instability) more than offsets the authorities' attempts to reduce demand by a large rise in interest rates (required by the interest-insensitivity of the curve).

The experience of UK monetary control in recent years suggests that the demand for bank lending is neither particularly interest-sensitive nor stable. This is discussed further in Chapter 6 where we examine the successes and failures of recent monetary policy. Here we suggest a number of reasons in principle why this may be so.

Firstly, in the short-run at least, a rise in interest rates will have

MONEY MARKETS

Rates ease

UK clearing bank base lending rate 9½ per cent (since June 14)

UK interest rates showed further falls yesterday reflecting increased market optimism over the possibility of a cut in base rates. Discount houses met little success in trying to drive down Bank of England dealing rates, with the latter resorting to repurchase agreements in order to meet the market shortage. The Bank forecast a shortage of around £350m with factors affecting the market including maturing assistance and a take up of Treasury bills—£393m and a rise in the note circulation of £220m. On the other hand Exchequer transactions added £214m to the system.

Morning assistance was confined to purchases of £8m of eligible bank bills in band 2 (15-33 days) at 9½ per cent with a further £358m in the afternoon comprising purchases of £65m of eligible bank bills in band 2 at 9½ per cent. The Bank also entered into sale and repurchase agreements on £293m of bills at $9\frac{11}{16}$-9¾ per cent, unwinding on September 30, and also provided a round of late assistance of £25m. Total help amounted to £391m.

In the interbank market week-end money opened at 9¾-10¼ per cent and eased initially to 10-10¼ per cent before coming back to 10½ per cent and then easing to 9 per cent. Late balances were taken at 10½ per cent however.

LONDON MONEY RATES

Sept. 23 1983	Sterling Certificate of deposit	Interbank	Local Authority deposits	Local Auth. negotiable bonds	Finance House Deposits	Company Deposits	Discount Market Deposits	Treasury Bills Φ	Eligible Bank Bills Φ	Fine Trade Bills Φ
Overnight	—	9-10½	10	—	—	9½-10¼	9-10	—	—	—
2 days notice	—	—	9¾-9⅞	—	—	—	—	—	—	—
7 days or	—	—	—	—	—	10¼	—	—	—	—
7 days notice	—	9⅞-10¼	9¾-9⅞	—	—	—	9½-9¾	—	—	—
One month	$9\frac{13}{16}$-$9\frac{11}{16}$	9¾-9⅞	9¾	9⅞-9⅝	9¾	10⅛	9⅜	9½	9⅛	10⅛
Two months	9⅝-9½	9⅝-9¾	$9\frac{11}{16}$	9⅞-9⅝	9⅝	10	9⅛	$9\frac{7}{32}$-9¼	$9\frac{3}{16}$-$9\frac{7}{32}$	$9\frac{27}{32}$
Three months	9½-9⅜	9½-$9\frac{11}{16}$	9⅝	10-9⅝	9⅝	9⅞	9	$8\frac{15}{16}$-9	$9\frac{1}{16}$-$9\frac{3}{32}$	$9\frac{23}{32}$
Six months	$9\frac{7}{16}$-9⅜	9½-$9\frac{11}{16}$	9⅝	9⅜-9	9⅝	—	—	—	9	9⅝
Nine months	9½-$9\frac{13}{32}$	9⅝-$9\frac{13}{16}$	9⅝	9⅞-9½	9¾	—	—	—	—	—
One year	9½-$9\frac{7}{16}$	9¾-$9\frac{15}{16}$	9¾-9⅞	10-9⅝	$9\frac{15}{16}$	—	—	—	—	—
Two years	—	—	10½-10¾	—	—	—	—	—	—	—

ECGD Fixed Rate Export Scheme IV. Average Rate for interest period August 3 to September 6 1983 (inclusive) 9.930 per cent.

Local authorities and finance houses seven days' notice others seven days fixed. Long-term local authority mortgage rates nominally three years 11 per cent; four years 11¼-11½ per cent; five years 11¼-11½ per cent. ΦBank bill rates in table are buying rates for prime paper. Buying rates for four months' bank bills $9\frac{1}{16}$-$9\frac{3}{32}$ per cent; four months' trade bills $9\frac{23}{32}$ per cent.

Approximate selling rate for one-month Treasury bills 9¼-$9\frac{7}{16}$ per cent; two months 9⅛ per cent and three months $8\frac{13}{16}$-8⅞ per cent. Approximate selling rate for one month bank bills $9\frac{7}{16}$-$9\frac{13}{32}$ per cent; two months $9\frac{1}{16}$-9⅛ per cent and three months $8\frac{15}{16}$-9 per cent; trade bills 9⅞ per cent; two months $9\frac{19}{32}$ per cent and three months $9\frac{15}{32}$ per cent.

Finance Houses Base Rate (published by the Finance Houses Association) 10 per cent from September 1, 1983. London and Scottish Clearing Bank Rates for lending 9½ per cent. London Deposit Rates for sums at seven days' notice 6 per cent.

Treasury Bills: Average tender rates of discount 8.9826 per cent. Certificates of Tax Deposit (Series 6). Deposits of £100,000 and over held under one month 9¾ per cent; one-three months 9¾ per cent; three-six months 10 per cent; six-12 months 10¼ per cent. Under £100,000 9½ per cent from September 13. Deposits held under Series 4-5 10 per cent. The rates for all deposits withdrawn for cash 8 per cent.

Fig. 4.13

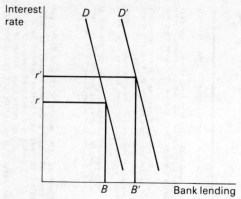

Fig. 4.14

its effect mainly upon **proposed** borrowing. If the cost goes up, firms and households planning expenditures using borrowed funds may be deterred from going ahead. On the other hand, the planning process may be such that it is more expensive for firms to abandon well-advanced plans than it is for them to put up with the now higher interest payments. Indeed, they may have to borrow more than originally planned to take account of the higher interest payments they will have to make. Certainly, there is little which those with existing loans, taken out at lower interest rates and already used or committed, can do to increase their repayments. Net indebtedness may continue to grow.

Secondly, as we have explained in Chapter 2, if borrowers believe the new interest rates to be historically high and likely to fall again soon, the kinds of loans offered by banks – short-term, variable interest rate – will seem more attractive than long-term fixed interest bonds. If, as a result, firms switch from borrowing in the corporate bond market to borrowing from banks, this will be a source of **increase** in the money stock.

Thirdly, if the rise in interest rate occurs at a time when corporate liquidity is being squeezed by falling sales – as in a period of recession, or because of reductions in government spending on aid to industry – firms may be forced into 'distress borrowing' whatever the level of interest rates. They simply have to borrow short in order to meet their bills.

Finally, it has to be remembered that the investment plans of firms and households to borrow to buy consumer durables will be plans to buy physical assets, the prices of which will be rising with inflation. Thus inflation may lead to increases in money value of loans sought. Further, if it is thought that inflation will continue at a high rate, firms and households may be more willing to go into debt than might otherwise be the case. The government may be pushing up nominal interest rates, but **real** interest rates (after allowing for expected inflation) may be falling. In these circumstances the demand curve for bank lending may be shifting progressively to the right.

When the government announces a target rate of monetary growth of, say, 10 per cent per annum, it hopes to set interest rates, its borrowing requirement and debt sales at levels which, given the rate of inflation, will produce a rate of growth in the money supply of 10 per cent. Clearly, if they underestimate the rate of inflation or if, for any other of the above reasons, firms respond differently to the increased interest rate than expected, the money supply growth will exceed the target rate. It is plain that precise control of bank lending to the non-bank private sector is very difficult.

Neither is it easy to control precisely public sector bank borrowing. Firstly, the government may underestimate its own borrowing needs. The PSBR is not itself an instrument for which the authorities can simply choose a value. Governments may decide upon tax **rates** and levels of some types of expenditure, but the total tax **yield** and the level of total expenditure will depend also upon the level of economic activity and the rate of inflation. For example, in a recession, the PSBR will, **ceteris paribus**, tend to increase. It is always possible for the actual PSBR to differ from that projected and if debt sales and interest rates have been set according to the needs of a lower figure, the need for residual or monetary financing will be that much greater. This will also happen, even if the PSBR is correctly forecast, if the authorities subsequently encounter difficulties in selling government debt to the non-bank private sector. If would-be purchasers of gilt-edged stock fear that future interest rate rises are likely, and this is obviously possible in a period of 'tight' monetary policy, they will simultaneously fear a capital loss on any bonds they may buy. If this fear results in lower than planned gilt sales, again the authorities will have to resort to monetary methods of financing the borrowing.

The last group of problems arises because of certain costs associated with using interest-baséd methods of control. Clearly, any system of control which the authorities adopt carries with it the implication that the system will, when necessary, be used. This hardly seems worth saying. However, there are particularly high costs, in the form of a conflict of aims, which attach to interest rate policy.

Firstly, as we have seen, 'tight' money requires 'high' interest rates both to damp down the private sector demand for bank credit and to maximise the sale of gilt-edged stock. Governments have always been sensitive about raising interest rates, however. Partly, this may be due to the political unpopularity which is thought to come from the eight million households who are currently buying their homes with the aid of a mortgage; partly, the argument is that high interest rates discourage investment; and partly also because issuing government stock when interest rates are high means that the government is committed to making large interest payments for some years to come. The need to 'depoliticise', to distance the government from unpopular movements in interest rates, was a subsidiary reason for the abolition in 1981 of official announcements of Minimum Lending Rate.

Secondly, a conflict may arise with exchange rate policy. International capital movements between the developed countries are frequent and large, and some of the capital is of a very short-term nature, flowing into a country to buy financial assets when the return looks comparatively favourable. Clearly, a rise in interest rates, other things being equal, will tend to encourage an inflow. With a fixed exchange rate the authorities will be able to maintain the rate only by supplying unlimited quantities of the domestic currency at the official price. This, in itself, tends to increase the money stock which the high interest rates were intended to reduce. Under a floating exchange rate regime, however, the demand for the domestic currency will push up its price, thereby cheapening imports and reducing the competitiveness of export industries. In a period of recession in particular, such an appreciation of the exchange rate would be unwelcome to the government which may, in consequence be deterred from raising interest rates as promptly or as far as the level required for effective monetary control.

APPENDIX   Public sector borrowing and the money supply

If the public sector borrows from the monetary sector and spends the funds it borrows, the recipients of those funds deposit them with their banks: the money stock has increased. Thus, as we said in Section 4.4, there is a connection between public sector borrowing and changes in the money stock. When it came to power in 1979, the Conservative government stressed the need to reduce the PSBR as a means of controlling the rate of monetary growth; this, in turn, as a means of reducing the rate of inflation. This was clearly stated in a white paper. **The Government's Expenditure Plans 1980–81** (Cmnd 7746). 'It is essential to contain and reduce progressively the growth of the money supply. This means that Government borrowing must in turn be firmly controlled. It is a main determinant of monetary growth.'

However, we know that it is only that part of public sector borrowing that is financed by borrowing from the monetary sector which adds to the money stock (monetary financing). Selling debt to the non-bank private sector only redistributes the existing stock. The present government, however, has often argued that there are still 'monetary' consequences, in that persuading people to hold more debt means selling debt at progressively higher interest rates, or at least at interest rates which are higher than they would otherwise have been. If **this** happens, the money stock will not have been increased but some private sector investment will have been discouraged or 'crowded-out' by the higher interest rates. In Chapter 6 we look at the efforts that have been made to reduce the PSBR to avoid these consequences, and at the difficulties involved in so doing. In this appendix we want to look at the evidence for the assertion that the PSBR has had adverse monetary consequences in recent years. We look at four things: firstly, the proportion of the PSBR financed by monetary means; secondly, the ratio of monetary financing to total monetary growth; thirdly, the course of interest rates on government bonds; and, finally, at recent developments in debt marketing. Table 4.4 contains most of the details.

From cols (1), (3) and (5), it is apparent that there is no obvious relationship between the **size** of the PSBR and the **proportion** of it which is financed by monetary means. If anything, the proportion financed in this way has tended to fall in recent years,

107

Table 4.4 Public sector borrowing and the money supply

Date	PSBR (£bn.)	Sales of debt to non-banks (£bn)	Monetary financing (1) – (2)	$\triangle £M_3$ (£bn.)	(3) ÷ (1)	(3) ÷ (4)	r*
	(1)	(2)	(3)	(4)	(5)	(6)	(7)
1975–76	10.6	5.3	5.3	2.5	0.50	2.12	14.39
1976–77	8.5	7.2	1.3	3.1	0.15	0.42	14.43
1977–78	5.5	6.6	–1.1	5.9	—	–0.19	12.73
1978–79	9.2	8.5	0.7	5.4	0.08	0.01	12.47
1979–80	9.9	9.2	0.7	7.1	0.07	0.01	12.99
1980–81	13.2	8.9	4.3	10.7	0.32	0.40	13.79
1981–82	8.8	7.0	1.8	17.5	0.20	0.10	14.75
1982–83	9.2	9.0	0.2	9.7	0.02	0.02	12.88

* Average redemption yield on twenty-year bonds.

Sources: *Financial Statistics*, HMSO (various issues), Table 2.6; *Economic Trends*, HMSO (various issues), Tables 52, 66; Llewellyn *et al.* (1982) Ch. 3

even when the PSBR has been growing. Taking the period as a whole, there have been substantial variations in the proportion of PSBR financed by monetary means. In 1977–78 monetary financing was negative as a result of successful bond sales to the non-bank private sector.

Nor is it any easier to argue that the amount of monetary financing that has occurred is closely related to the overall growth of £M_3. In 1975–76 monetary financing was very large indeed, equal in fact to twice the overall increase in £M_3. Since then, monetary financing has been equivalent to only a very small and unstable proportion of the total change in £M_3.

If monetary financing is only a small proportion of PSBR and bears only a small and uncertain relation to overall monetary growth, this is evidence of the authorities' success in financing it by non-monetary means; that is, by selling debt to to the non-bank private sector. This, it is argued by those who wish to reduce the PSBR, leads to 'high' interest rates which inhibit some elements of private sector investment. For this argument to be completely persuasive, evidence is needed of the interest-elasticity of investment expenditure. This requirement apart, however, the argument faces some difficulty in its earlier stages given the observed pattern of debt sales and the interest rate on long-dated bonds (cols (2) and (7)). Since 1975–76 bond rates have fallen, though their course has been erratic. On the other hand, debt sales have increased, though again the path is far from smooth. Most significantly, the two years of largest debt sales (1978–79 and 1979–80) were years when interest rates were at their lowest, and expressed as **real** rates (nominal rates minus the expected rate of price inflation) could even be thought to have been negative. Of course, it is always possible to argue that whatever the level of interest rates that **actually** prevailed, in the absence of such debt sales they **would have been lower**. There is no falsifying assertions of that kind. For exactly the same reasons, they can never be proved. The argument that private sector investment has been inhibited by the failure of real interest rates to be even more negative than they have actually been (even before allowing for tax relief) takes some believing.

How is it that large quantities of public sector debt have been sold in recent years without a secular rise in interest rates? A complete answer would have to look at many factors determining the attractiveness of public sector debt relative to other types of financial asset: comparative yields, capital gains/losses, tax treatment and so on, as well as at changes in the overall level of saving out of income which the community wishes to undertake. All we wish to note here is that **some** part of the success in selling debt without obvious interest rate consequences is due to imaginative changes in the type of debt offered and in the way in which it has been marketed.

Take gilt-edged stock (marketable debt) first. Since 1977, four new types of debt have become available. In 1977 the public was first able to subscribe to a 'partly paid' stock by making an initial payment followed by two further instalments, usually within three months. Many partly paid issues have since been made, their success resting on people's being able to buy them at a time when they are temporarily short of sufficient liquid funds to buy them outright. Less successful but also introduced in 1977, have been the issues of variable-rate stock. More recently, in 1982, index-linked stocks were made available to all purchasers, having initially been restricted to pension funds and life insurance companies. In 1982 and 1983 the authorities issued a number of low-coupon, short-dated stocks which offered subscribers a relatively low yield, but the certainty of a tax-free capital gain at the time of redemption.

All of these innovations in the type of stock on offer have to be seen against a significant change also in the method of selling. Before 1979, the invariable practice was to offer stock for sale at an announced price, predetermined to make the stock attractive, given current market conditions. On occasions, this fixed price would fail to clear the stock and the Bank of England would be left with unsold stock which it would subsequently release onto the market as and when conditions suggested the price would be acceptable. This was known as the 'tap' method of selling. Since 1979, the authorities have moved toward a 'partial-tender' system where stock is announced for sale by tender, allowing the market to fix the price which will clear the stock. This is subject to a minimum tender price (hence **partial**-tender) designed to prevent a sudden collapse of stock prices in the event of the authorities miscalculating the timing and attractiveness of the sale. The main argument in favour of such a system is that if the minimum price is set realistically, the authorities can be certain of selling given quantities of debt at predetermined intervals. This certainty should allow a closer correlation of non-bank borrowing with expenditure and thus reduce the need for monetary financing.

The expression 'non-marketable debt' refers to what is more popularly known as National Savings. This is clearly another way for the general public to lend to the government but the assets acquired (National Savings Certificates, for example) cannot be bought and sold directly between members of the public. In recent years, non-marketable debt has made an important contribution to the financing of the PSBR. In 1981–82, net sales of non-marketable debt amounted to nearly 40 per cent of the PSBR compared with around 5 per cent in the mid-1970s. The main innovations are well known. The introduction of index-linked 'Save-As-You-Earn' facilities and the extension of eligibility for ownership of index-linked National Savings Certificates have been spectacular successes but their growth has been very closely paralleled by deposits in the National Savings Bank Investment Account which, since 1977, has offered a near money-market rate of interest in return for one month's notice of withdrawal.

Whether the authorities' ingenuity in finding new forms of debt attractive to the non-bank private sector will continue, one cannot know. It is, of course, possible that at some future point the remarkable depth of the UK market for public sector debt will be reached. Nonetheless, arguments which stress the undesirable monetary consequences of a given size of PSBR have to be based upon what, in fact, has happened. As yet, the evidence of damage is unconvincing.

QUESTIONS

Essay questions

1. Explain why in the context of the British monetary system the authorities must choose between controlling the prices of government bonds and controlling the money supply. (JMB).

2. How does the government influence the supply of money in the UK? Explain how monetary policy can be used to reduce the level of aggregate demand. (JMB).

3. What are the main components of the UK supply of money? Why might the authorities wish to control the money supply and how effectively can they do so? (L)

4. Outline the present functions of the London discount market. To what extent has the role of the discount market within the financial system changed since 1970? (I of B)

5. What different techniques are available to the monetary authorities when seeking to control the money supply? Assess critically the effectiveness of each type of control. (I of B).

Discussion questions

1. Why does the elasticity of demand for bank lending matter in monetary control?

2. What is meant by 'portfolio shifts'? What is their relevance to monetary control?

3. What is meant by 'disintermediation'?

4. What difficulties confront a system of monetary base control?

FURTHER READING

Many texts deal with bank credit multipliers. Good examples of those which do so explicitly are Vane and Thompson (1979) and Bain (1982). Others, like Lipsey (1983) Ch. 38, discuss the importance of reserve assets in a way which assumes some multiplier relationship between reserves and bank deposits. Multiplier analyses of changes in the money stock should only be read, however, alongside Llewellyn *et al.* (1982) Ch. 2, who are severely critical of this type of approach in particular for its ignoring of the demand for bank deposits. The best sources on interest rate control and direct controls are Brown (1981, 1982) and for a comprehensive survey of monetary control in the 1970s, Gowland (1982) is very useful. A valuable insight into the day-to-day (almost hour-by-hour) operations of the Bank of England in the money market is in *BEQB*, March 1982. The connection between PSBR, monetary growth and interest rates is examined by Llewellyn *et al.* (1982) Chs 3 and 8.

5 THE DEMAND FOR MONEY

We have seen in Chapter 4 that attempts to control the money supply work through the impact of interest rate changes on the **demand for bank loans**. Changes in the money supply will then influence the rest of the economy through portfolio shifts arising because the altered money supply is now different from the amount of money demanded. The size of these effects will depend crucially on the nature of the demand for money. Particularly important will be the relationship between the **demand for money** and the interest rate.

5.1 THE IMPORTANCE OF THE DEMAND FOR MONEY

We can explain the importance of the connection between the rate of interest and the demand for money best by returning to our old friend $MV = PT$. We earlier explained that for changes in the money stock (M) to be directly associated with changes occurring on the right-hand side of the equation (i.e. changes in nominal income) the velocity of circulation (V) must be constant or, at least, predictable.

Now assume we have induced a fall in the supply of money through increasing interest rates in the economy. If people wish to continue to hold the same amount of money as previously they will attempt to maintain their balances of it by reducing their demand for other assets, including consumer durables and capital equipment. Nominal income will then fall and this will act to bring the demand for money balances into line with the now smaller stock of money. If, indeed, the **only** reason why people reduce their demand for money is because nominal income has fallen, we shall only return to an equilibrium with the demand for money equal to the money supply when PT has fallen in proportion to the fall in M (i.e. V is constant).

On the other hand, if the interest rate rise needed to bring about the required fall in the money supply **also** causes people to wish to hold smaller money balances, then PT may need to fall by less than the fall in the money supply in order to take us back to equilibrium. That is, V will have risen, partly offsetting the fall in M. The stronger the relationship between interest rate and the demand for money, the more V will change.

It remains true that as long as the relationship between interest rate and the demand for money is **known**, it might be possible, through adjusting interest rate, to know what would happen to both the money supply and to nominal income. However, we can only know the future strength of a relationship if we have reason to believe that it will stay the same as it now is, or will change in predictable ways. If the relationship between interest rate and the demand for money is unstable, then setting targets for M will be a very risky way of attempting to achieve desired levels of PT.

5.1.1 Idle balances and the velocity of circulation

Another approach to the argument about velocity is to remind ourselves that V can be defined simply as the number of times which, on average, a unit of money turns over (i.e. is used) in a given time period. We can think about the notion of this average by considering the money stock as being held by people in the economy either as active balances or as idle balances. Active money balances are held because people feel they need them to undertake transactions. Indeed, the purpose of holding such balances is to make them 'turn over' in the purchase of commodities. Idle balances are not intended to be so used and are held because people regard money as a safe or a flexible way of holding part of their wealth.

If there is a given money stock, it is clear that the smaller the proportion of it which is held idle, other things being equal, the more often the average unit of money will turn over (i.e. the higher the velocity of circulation will be). Thus, if in our example the rise in interest rates which causes the money supply to fall also causes the proportion of it held as idle balances to fall, velocity will increase.

Further, if there are frequent autonomous changes in the amount of money held idle (for instance, due to changes in confidence about the future), velocity will not be constant and will be more difficult to predict.

5.1.2 A more formal expression

We can express this in the jargon of economics by saying that we wish to know the interest elasticity of the demand for money and whether the demand for money function (the relationship between the demand for money and the major variables influencing it) is stable.

This can be seen to relate very closely to our discussion in Chapter 2 since, as with any other commodity, the demand for money will be price-inelastic (i.e. interest-rate-inelastic) if there are not good substitutes for it – the position which we characterised as being that of monetarists.

As we shall see, the issue of the stability of the demand for money function raises questions regarding the degree of uncertainty in the economy and responses to that uncertainty.

To consider this issue we must look more formally than we have so far done at why people choose to hold money rather than other assets. Most of this discussion is in terms of the stock of money demanded and supplied, but we need to remember that government monetary targets are in the form of percentage rates of change in the target variable.

5.2 APPROACHES TO THE DEMAND FOR MONEY

The usual approach to the demand for money is through three motives which people are said to have for holding money – transactions, precautionary and speculative. These can easily be reduced to two by amalgamating the transactions and precautionary motives. Then our two remaining motives can be identified with our two views of money from Chapter 2.

There we showed that the first view (which we align with the transactions motive or the demand for active balances) derives from concentration on the use of money for purchasing goods or settling debts and leads to the view that there are no assets which are good substitutes for money. The second view (which we align with the speculative motive) stresses the liquidity of assets and leads to the proposition that there are many good substitutes for money.

This is all very well; but why should one group of economists think of money in one way, and another group think of it in a quite different way?

5.2.1 Keynesians and uncertainty

The Keynesian approach arises from a stress by them on uncertainty in the operation of an economy and on the impact of uncertainty on people's behaviour. If people cannot know future demand for products, future prices, etc., they will feel much less secure about investment and consumption decisions, many of which (especially investment decisions) depend upon estimates of what will happen in the future. In an uncertain world, the argument continues, people will hold a higher proportion of their wealth in forms which are denominated in money terms; above all, they will hold more assets which have a reasonably certain money value or which can easily be turned into money if there is an apparent increase in the risk of loss. Uncertainty gives people a preference for liquidity.

Such a view also disposes economists to be concerned with planned expenditure and the relationship between plans and outcomes. In formulating plans, it is liquidity which is important, not holdings of narrowly defined money which must ultimately be acquired for purchases to be made.

5.2.2 Monetarists and equilibrium

The monetarist view, however, comes from an assumption that the economy and individual markets within it can be assumed to be in equilibrium or tending strongly towards it. If the economy is in equilibrium (or, more strictly, is subject only to small, random movements around equilibrium values), the problem of uncertainty is removed. People know the set of equilibrium prices ruling in markets, or behave as if they know them. Their past estimates of what would be likely to happen in the economy have been vindicated by events and there is no reason for them to change their behaviour. Money is not needed as a protection against uncertainty. Instead, people's motives within markets can be viewed in real or opportunity cost terms.

A decision to buy one brand of cornflakes involves a comparison between it and other **things** which we could have instead. The only roles for money in such a world are to allow comparisons to be made and to enable transactions to be carried out efficiently (avoiding the waste of time and effort involved in barter). The Keynesian possibility that people may choose to hold money idle rather than to spend it on goods or services disappears. In the purest form of the monetarist model, money has no value in itself. It is **only** a medium of exchange.

We are not interested here in the relationship between planned and actual expenditure since people's plans are always assumed to be fulfilled.

5.2.3 Why equilibrium?

Why, you may ask, assume that the economy is in equilibrium? Doing so is an expression of belief in the strength of market forces and in the efficiency of the market system. If one is convinced that powerful forces operate to bring demand into line with supply (i.e. to clear markets), it is not unreasonable to analyse the economy as always being in a state of equilibrium (continuous market-clearing, as it is called these days).

The Keynesian response is the straightforward one that some important markets (especially the labour market) do not clear and that the real world is one of disequilibrium and uncertainty.

How does one choose between these two views of the nature of markets? One way is to try to find out from people's behaviour whether they are acting **as if** the economy is in equilibrium and only holding money as active balances for transactions purposes or **as if** the world is an uncertain one and are holding money also to attempt to reduce the possibility of loss.

This is very difficult to do. Although various measures of the stock of money at different times in the past are available, the demand for money itself cannot be measured directly. We may know the amounts of notes and coin and bank deposits held at a particular time, but not whether those amounts were what people wanted to hold. The simplest thing to do is to assume that money markets are in equilibrium and that the measured money supply is always equal to the demand for money. That is what is usually done for the purposes of testing money demand functions, but it is far from being completely satisfactory.

5.3 DEMAND FOR MONEY FUNCTIONS

Accept, however, that little else can be done. The next step is to return to our two basic motives and derive from them those variables which seem most likely to influence the demand for money. Firstly, let us consider the proposition that there is a constant relationship between the value of transactions which people wish to undertake and the amount of money they need to hold to undertake them. Such a constant relationship does not seem improbable, but we need to make a number of assumptions.

5.3.1 The transactions motive

The usual starting point is to propose that the value of commodities purchased and debt settled will be related to income – other things being equal, the higher income is, the more people will wish to spend, and the more money they will need to carry out their spending plans. The only point of dispute here relates to the interpretation of 'income'.

It is possible simply to propose current income as the relevant variable. This has the compelling advantage that national income can be directly measured. However, the constraint on people's ability to purchase assets is wealth rather than current income. We have discussed the difficulties involved in measuring wealth in Chapter 2 and have pointed out that the most common answers are:

(a) to take government debt plus the value of corporate sector assets as a measure of private sector non-human wealth; and
(b) to use permanent income as a proxy for all wealth, including human wealth.

Since permanent income itself cannot be measured directly (depending as it does on people's expectations about the future) it has to be estimated from present and past income levels.

Most money demand functions use one or other of these variables, with the choice made seeming to have very little effect on the results.

5.3.2 The significance of institutional arrangements

It is obvious that the reason for needing to hold money over time in order to undertake transactions is that receipts of income occur at different times from desired transactions. If we could make all our purchases at the instant we received our income, we would not need to hold money balances.

Thus, the amount people need to hold for this purpose will be influenced by the time pattern of receipts and expenditure in an economy. Receipt patterns change little, but expenditure patterns can and do change because they are affected by credit arrangements.

If one acquires goods over the course of a month by using a credit card and pays for them all with a single payment at the end of the month, one need hold money for this purpose only at the end of the month. One's average holdings of money are bound to be less than if one needed to pay separately for each good at imprecisely known times during the month. The very fact that one needs to convert other assets into money less often is going to make one more willing to put receipts into forms other than money.

Institutional arrangements can, then, affect the value of transactions undertaken with a given stock of money. The first point of interest is whether such changes in arrangements occur sufficiently often to damage the notion that the velocity of circulation is constant in the short run. It is quite easy to believe that they do not. In the longer run, as financial institutions become more sophisticated, we will expect velocity to increase steadily but fairly predictably.

What is more crucial is whether **existing** arrangements at any time allow a link between the size of the money supply and the amount people need to hold in order to undertake a particular value of transactions. If, for example, firms respond to a fall in the money stock by increasing the average length of trade credit, there will be a once-and-for-all increase in the velocity of circulation, partially (at least) offsetting the reduction in money supply.

It would not, of course, be reasonable to propose that adjustments of this kind could continue to be made in the face of continuing reductions in the money stock. It may also well be that the responses of firms to money stock changes may be sufficiently consistent for us still to be able to predict what will happen to velocity. However, the more flexible credit arrangements are, the more room for doubt there is as to whether the money supply is independent of the demand for money.

5.3.3 The precautionary motive

This relates to the willingness of people or firms to accept the consequences of not having adequate money to make the purchases they wish to, or to settle debts when required. Such consequences may range from embarrassment to bankruptcy. In one sense, money held for precautionary reasons is being held as an idle balance. The motive, however, is usually amalgamated with the demand for active balances because it is related to the desire to undertake transactions. It is best for us to keep the term idle balances' to refer to money balances held for speculative reasons.

In any case, since we can assume that the general attitude to this sort of risk changes little over time, we need not worry much about this factor from the point of view of monetary policy.

5.3.4 Transactions costs and interest rates

Next, we need to mention the transactions costs and possible capital losses involved in changing other assets into money in order for purchases to be made at the desired time. We must offset against such costs the income foregone in holding money instead of some other asset.

This will depend on rates of interest payable on alternative assets. We will expect the demand for money to be higher, the lower such interest rates are.

5.3.5 The importance of the price level

As prices rise, so does the value of transactions which people wish to undertake. By far the most common assumption is that the demand for money will increase, other things being equal, in proportion with increases in prices. Tests carried out on demand for money functions do seem to support this proposition.

Another way of expressing it is to say that we are interested in the demand for **real** money balances. That is, it is accepted that both sides of a demand for money equation can be divided by an index of the price level, leaving us with a demand for real money balances expressed as a function of variables denominated in real terms.

5.3.6 Expected inflation

Another complication, previously mentioned in Chapter 2, concerns expected inflation. The higher people expect the rate of inflation to be the more they will wish to hold real assets rather than financial assets. Money loses value in real terms during inflation. Thus, although the demand for money will be greater the higher the price level, it will be lower the higher the expected **rate** of inflation. To make complete sense of this you must remember the vital **other things being equal** qualification which must be appended to all such statements in economics.

Interest in the expected rate of inflation leads us to ask how people decide upon the likely future rate of inflation (that is, how their expectations of the future are formed). Several theories about this have been made use of in economics. The most common of these has been the approach known as adaptive expectations which assumes that people's views about the future are determined by the past and, perhaps, by the extent to which their past estimates of the future had turned out to be incorrect; that is, they adapt their views in the light of experience. An example of adaptive expectations which we have mentioned in this book is the calculation of permanent income as a weighted average of present and past income levels. One message from the adaptive expectations approach is that, in times of rapidly changing inflation rates, people's estimates of future inflation rates are likely to be incorrect.

If this is so, the demand for money will be different from what it would have been if people had **known** what the rate of inflation was going to be. What follows from that? Suppose the rate of growth of the money supply increases and assume, for the sake of argument, that this leads directly to an increase in the rate of inflation. However, people have based their demand for money on an expected lower rate of inflation. They will then find that they are holding less money than they wish to and will seek to exchange other assets for money. This will go on as long as expectations of the future rate of inflation turn out to be wrong. In other words, the money market will not be in equilibrium unless expectations are correct.

If we wish to analyse equilibrium positions, we can propose the idea that people will eventually learn to guess the future rate of inflation correctly. We can call the period of time necessary for this to happen the **long run**. In the long run, then, the money market will be in equilibrium and there will be no tendency for people to alter their behaviour. It is important to realise that this is merely a theoretical idea. There can be no answer to the question as to how long the long run is. It is very similar to the assumption of perfect information in the theory of perfect competition. It is not meant to be a description of the real world.

5.3.7 Rational expectations

In recent years, an alternative view of the formation of expectations has become popular. This begins with the unremarkable notion that people in markets make the best use of all available information. The problems arise in interpreting the phrases 'the best use' and 'all available information'.

In practice, this view (known as rational expectations) has come down to the idea that people can be assumed to know that the rate of inflation is determined directly by the rate of growth of the money supply and to know what that rate of growth is. This requires the assumption that governments can and do control the rate of growth of the money supply and that people know this to be the case and, hence, accept government announcements as to target rates of money supply growth as an accurate indication of future rates of inflation. What this does is to remove the distinction between the short run (when people's expectations are incorrect) and the long run. Under rational expectations, we are always in the long run and the economy is always in equilibrium. Again, this is not intended to be a description of the real world. The claim is rather that people's behaviour can best be predicted by assuming that they act as if the economy were always in equilibrium.

One implication of the adaptive expectations approach is that there are likely to be long time-lags between changes in the rate of growth of the money supply and changes in the rate of inflation because in the short run the relationship will be being disturbed by responses to incorrect expectations. The rational expectations view, on the other hand, implies that there will be no such time-lags.

5.3.8 Human capital

Our final point here relates to human capital. If our demand for money function includes permanent income, we will expect the demand for money to be greater, the higher human wealth is as a proportion of total wealth. We have explained this point previously in Section 2.5.5.

5.3.9 A summary of elements in demand for money functions

We can summarise this discussion by saying that it is common to see the demand for money as being influenced by the following variables:

permanent income or wealth
rates of return on assets other than money
the level of prices
the expected rate of increase of prices
the proportion human wealth is of total wealth.

5.4 THE SPECULATIVE MOTIVE

The principal ideas here have also already been thoroughly treated. We shall, however, recapitulate briefly.

We have said that money has attractions as an asset because it enables people to seize profitable market opportunities as well as to reduce the risk of loss associated with falling prices of financial assets. We have also looked at the demand for money as just one part of the general process of matching assets to liabilities, i.e. as one part of ensuring that assets are adequately liquid.

Although it adds little to the argument, the speculative demand for money is so widely treated using an example from Keynes that we really need to explain this here.

5.4.1 The normal rate of interest

The usual beginning is to assume that there are only two types of assets – *money*, which is representative of short-term highly liquid assets, and *bonds*, representative of long-term illiquid assets. The extreme form of the bond is the consol, a bond which never matures and is held in perpetuity in return for interest payments. The capital is never repaid. Given that the interest rates payable on bonds issued in the past are fixed, changes in interest rates on bonds currently being issued will affect the attractiveness of old bonds. Thus, if the interest rate on new bonds rises, old bonds become relatively less attractive, fewer people wish to buy them and their price falls.

The next step is to see that people who already hold bonds will make a capital loss on their bonds if interest rates in the economy generally rise. If, then, we think this likely to happen, we shall not wish to hold bonds but shall prefer to sell them now before interest rates go up and hold money (the only alternative asset in this model) instead. If we are correct and interest rates do rise, bond prices fall and we can buy back into bonds at the new lower price, making a profit on the deal. Of course, if we are wrong and interest rates fall we shall have made a loss. We shall lose even if interest rates do not change since we shall have given up the interest we were previously receiving on our bonds.

Now we need to consider why people might think interest rates will rise (i.e. how people form their expectations about future interest rates). Here we use a third interpretation of expectations – different from both adaptive and rational expectations – which is, that people maintain a view regarding the rate of interest likely to be sustained in an economy under existing conditions (the normal rate of interest). If the present rate is below what they think of as normal, their expectation will be that it will rise in the near future and so they will sell bonds and hold money instead.

The lower the rate of interest is, the greater will be the number of people who expect it to rise. Hence, the lower the interest rate, the greater will be the total demand for money in the economy.

There are several qualifications one might wish to make to this argument. For example, unless they are foolish, people will allow some margin for error in deciding on the normal rate. Consequently, they may be unsure on some occasions whether the interest rate will rise or fall. They may think that there is, say, a 60 per cent probability that interest rates will rise, a 30 per cent chance that they will remain unchanged, and a 10 per cent chance that they will fall. In such a case they would switch away from bonds to money but would continue to hold some bonds. How many bonds they continued to hold would depend on their attitude towards risk as well as on their estimate of what was likely to happen to interest rates.

Again, the model can easily allow for more than one interest rate and for more than two types of asset. As long as interest rates on different kinds of assets move broadly in the same direction, we can derive the same proposition as we did earlier – that the lower are current interest rates, the more money will be held in the form of idle balances.

5.4.2 The speculative motive: a summary

Putting this together with our previous statements, we arrive at two points of importance. We have a second reason for expecting the demand for money to be negatively related to interest rate. In addition, the nature of that relationship will depend on the **normal** rate of interest and the way in which that normal rate is arrived at.

Many monetarists stress the direct route of the change in money supply on expenditure and, hence, favour the theoretical proposition that there is no relationship between the rate of interest and the demand for money. However, the existence of such a relationship need not present insuperable problems to them. It will mean that money supply changes will need to be that much greater to produce the required effects on expenditure levels because of the consequential offsetting changes in velocity. Short, however, of the liquidity trap case where velocity changes completely offset changes in the money supply, it would be possible in theory to allow for this – as long, that is, as the relationship between interest rates and the demand for money is stable and, hence, the changes in velocity are predictable.

Thus, the real problems arise over the question of interest rate expectations, though it remains true that monetarists would prefer the demand for money to be interest-rate-inelastic. If the 'normal rate' of interest is itself highly volatile (i.e. people are very uncertain about the direction of future interest rate changes), the demand for money will not be stably related to interest rate changes and the velocity will not be predictable. Much depends, then, on how people form expectations about the future.

5.5 INTEREST RATES AND THE DEMAND FOR MONEY: THE EVIDENCE

There seems little room for doubt that the demand for money is interest-elastic. Many tests have been carried out for different countries, over different time periods, using different measures of money, different interest rates, different definitions of income and different statistical techniques. Almost all of them have shown a significant negative relationship between interest rates and the demand for money. There has been disagreement about the strength of the relationship, and the search continues for definitions of money which will produce low interest rate elasticities. Evidence that the relationship between interest rate and the demand for the wide monetary base (M_0) may not be very strong has been used to support the recent adoption of it as a monetary target.

Concerning the stability of the relationship between interest rate and the demand for money, there is much uncertainty. In the early 1970s, evidence seemed to provide strong support for the monetarist argument in favour of stability. More recent studies have cast doubt on that view. The evidence seems now to favour the proposition that, in Britain in the 1970s, the demand for money function was decidedly unstable, especially if £M_3 is used as the measure of money in the equation. Again, the government seems now to be pinning its hopes on M_0. One study has indicated that the relationship between interest rate and the demand for M_0 might be stable; but in this connection, readers should remember Goodhart's Law which we outlined in section 3.2. This raises the possibility that attempting to achieve target values of M_0 may destroy any apparently existing stability.

5.6 THE REVERSE CAUSAL CHAIN

As in Chapter 1, we have considered the relationship between the money supply and nominal income in terms of the possible effects of an initial change in the money stock. It is as well, therefore, to remind ourselves that the reverse possibility exists.

Let us assume that for some quite different reason (say an increase in business confidence) there is an increase in desired consumption or investment expenditure. People wishing to spend now find that their money balances are inadequate for their purposes. Assume, however, that it is possible to prevent the total money supply from rising. People compete for the now inadequate money supply by selling other financial assets. Prices of these assets fall and interest rates rise, acting to discourage consumption and investment expenditure. The increase in interest rates, however, also leads to a reduction in idle money balances; the existing money stock becomes more intensively used – that is, the velocity increases, allowing increased nominal income to be supported by the unchanged money stock.

A more likely case will be where banks respond to the changed climate by offering an increased volume of loans (accepting a variety of assets as security as people attempt to convert more of their wealth into money). Bank assets (loans) and liabilities (deposits) both rise. The money supply increases. In this case the money supply is said to be endogenous (i.e. its size is determined by changes in the economy rather than by the policy of the authorities).

The implication here is that the authorities allow the money supply to increase rather than impose direct controls or accept a high level of interest rates. There would seem to be little point in doing anything else if our story above, that fixing the money supply leads to variations in velocity, is correct. It is worth noting, however, that even if we accept the idea that the velocity of money is **constant**, the authorities will be free to allow the money supply to rise (and hence accept an increase in nominal income) rather than to accept the consequences of controlling the money supply which they may see as politically or socially undesirable. The money supply may then become endogenous by virtue of government policy.

In a similar way, in an open economy, the money supply may become endogenous because the government accepts a system of fixed or managed exchange rates. Any increase in foreign exchange reserves produces an increase in the money supply. Equally, a fall in foreign exchange reserves will be associated with a fall in the money supply.

5.7 THE COSTS OF INFLATION AND THE DEMAND FOR MONEY

There has been much debate in recent years about the cost to an economy of persistent inflation. The argument usually proceeds by dividing inflation into unanticipated and anticipated inflation.

The costs of unanticipated inflation relate to the fact that, to some extent at least, people are ignorant of future rates of inflation and so are not able to organise their affairs fully to take into account rising prices. The costs then are arbitrary redistributions of income and losses of output and employment which may arise from the uncertainty generated by inflation.

However, since monetarist models largely deal with equilibrium or long-run positions in which it can be assumed that the rate of inflation is known, they are particularly concerned with the costs of anticipated inflation – those that might still be expected to arise even if people were able to adjust their activities completely to actual price rises.

The interesting thing, from our point of view, is that the major cost associated with anticipated inflation is related to the demand for money and the nature of money. Thus, one can argue that as inflation rates rise and money interest rates rise to preserve their real value, the demand for money will fall. Inflation will push people into holding assets other than money. This means that they will either have to spend more time and energy converting other assets into money when it is needed for purchases, or that there will be a tendency to move away from the use of money in exchange back towards barter. In either case there is seen to be a loss in welfare for individual people and for the economy as a whole.

The important question, though, is how big might one expect this loss to be. The answer clearly depends on the resolution of our old issue as to whether there are good substitutes for money. Keynesians may well say that because there are many very good substitutes for money, being pushed into holding them instead of money involves no great loss – certainly not enough to justify arguments that inflation is a greater problem than unemployment for economies. Different views of money and of the nature of a monetary economy remain central to many of the vital debates within economics.

QUESTIONS

Essay questions

1. The demand for money is normally inversely related to the rate of interest. How would you explain this relationship? (L)

2. Outline the factors that are likely to influence the community's demand for money. Why is this concept an important element of macroeconomic theory? (WJEC)

3. What determines the demand for money? How is this demand affected by inflation? (L)

4. What factors determine the demand for money? Analyse the ways in which a change in the rate of interest might affect this demand. (L)

5. Explain why the theory of the demand for money differs from the theory of the demand for anything else. (L)

Discussion questions

1. Why might the demand for a narrow measure of money be less interest-elastic than the demand for a broad measure of money?

2. Explain how the stability of money demand functions is related to the predictability of the velocity of money.

3. Explain what is meant by an 'exogenous' money supply and by an 'endogenous' money supply?

4. What is the difference between the demand for bank lending and the demand for money?

129

FURTHER READING

A useful treatment of the demand for money including empirical evidence up to the date of publication is Laidler (1977). Other sources at a higher level are Vane and Thompson (1979), Pierce and Shaw (1974) and Dennis (1981). Chapters 5 and 7 of Llewellyn *et al.* (1982) also contain valuable material. A good summary of demand for money studies up until 1979 is included in Artis and Lewis (1981). Havrilesky and Boorman (1980) contains a long chapter on demand for money functions which possesses a thorough bibliography of the American literature on the topic. Extracts from original papers on monetary theory by Friedman, Tobin and Hahn are in Surrey (1976). A recent study of the demand for narrow money aggregates is Johnston (1984)

More general macroeconomic texts which deal with demand for money functions include Westaway and Weyman-Jones (1977), Greenaway and Shaw (1983) and Challen *et al.* (1984).

6 THE RECENT CONDUCT OF MONETARY POLICY

6.1 THE RISE OF MONETARY POLICY

Several factors combined to produce the resurgence of interest in monetary policy in the 1970s. Some were practical: the difficulties involved in attempting to control credit in the 1960s and the monetary experiences of the Heath government in the 1970s certainly contributed. Some were related to policy problems, especially the emergence of inflation as a major concern from 1973 onwards and the coexistence of high levels of unemployment with high rates of inflation. Academic research played a role, particularly in producing evidence apparently showing stability of the velocity of circulation of money, leading to a much increased faith in the idea that controlling the money supply could have a strong impact on the level of money national income.

External influences on the British economy were also relevant. The floating of the exchange rate in June 1972 increased the possibility that the money supply could be controlled by the Bank of England. The International Monetary Fund, itself influenced by changed academic attitudes, helped to push Britain in the direction of setting money supply targets in the middle 1970s.

Finally, political ideology was involved. The form of the development of interest in monetary policy was associated with a renewed belief in the superiority of private market institutions over government ones and a change in attitude towards the causes of unemployment. These changes, which occurred everywhere in the western world, were much greater than could be explained by the findings of economic research.

Let us look at these points in more detail.

6.1.1 The experience of the Heath government

The difficulties which had occurred during the 1960s, when the monetary authorities had attempted to regulate the amount of credit in the economy through the use of direct controls on banks, had led to a desire for reform. The Heath government, when it came to power in 1970, wished to foster greater competition and so the 1971 Competition and Credit Control policy removed quantitative lending restrictions from banks. Since the government also wanted to be able to influence monetary growth to some extent, it was willing to have interest rates move up and down rather more than had been the case. That is, there was to be free competition for funds but the Bank of England was to use interest rates to try to ensure that the resulting growth of the money supply was in line with the government's aims.

The government also, however, was attempting to produce a rapid rate of growth of output (5 per cent per annum) and tried to achieve this by a consumer boom encouraged by a very expansionary budget in 1972. Further, as a preliminary to Britain's becoming a member of the EEC, the government wanted to join the European fixed exchange rate system known as 'the snake in the tunnel'. The attempt to do so was very short-lived and its failure led to the floating of sterling in 1972. One result of all these policies was an embarrassingly rapid rate of growth of the domestic money supply – a growth of 60 per cent occurring in $£M_3$ between December 1971 and December 1973.

This large increase had not been checked by the qualitative advice regarding lending given by the Bank of England nor by quite sizeable increases in interest rates. Something had to give. What gave was the free competition among banks. Direct controls in the form of the Supplementary Special Deposits scheme ('the corset') reappeared in December 1973. Other modifications in the 1970s led to the system becoming complex and difficult to manage once again and to renewed calls for reform, particularly for a further attempt to bring competition back into money markets.

6.1.2 The emergence of inflation

The expansionary policies of the government no doubt added to existing inflationary pressures from international sources. The fall in the sterling exchange rate following floating in 1972, and the rise in world raw materials prices made things worse. The large oil price rise of late 1973 added to the strength of the now inevitable rapid increase in the rate of inflation. The form of the prices and incomes policy of the Heath government merely served to intensify the inflationary pressures by allowing wages throughout the economy to rise in line with increases in import prices.

The Wilson government which followed then used demand policies to try to limit domestic unemployment in the face of the decline in competitiveness of the economy caused by the oil price rise. The combination of events and policies led to the unprecedented rates of inflation experienced by the British economy (rising to 23 per cent in 1974).

The emergence of inflation as a major problem drew more attention to monetary conditions. Monetary policy had always been thought to be likely to be of most importance in times of rapidly rising prices. The notion of inflation being caused by the existence of too much money has for long been a powerful one in the minds both of economists and of members of the public and this was reinforced by the rapid rate of growth of the money supply during the term of the Heath government.

Also, the existence together of high unemployment and high inflation (stagflation) undermined the Keynesian view that very high rates of inflation were likely only at high levels of demand and employment. Keynesian post-war demand policies principally using fiscal policy were seen to have 'failed'. The idea that it had been such policies which had been responsible for the long boom of the 1950s and 1960s started to appear unconvincing.

Keynesians, of course, had contributed to their own demise by making rather too grand claims for the success of their policies. Insistence that economies need never again face major recessions such as that of the 1930s because governments had learned the secret of demand management were all very well until stagflation occurred. When that did occur, the Kéynesian position was drastically weakened.

6.1.3 The role of academic research

Meanwhile, as we mentioned at the end of Chapter 5, considerable academic research had supported the proposition that the relationship between interest rates and the demand for money was stable over time. We have shown that this is just another way of saying that the velocity of money is predictable. Thus, if the government could control the money supply it could hope to influence, with some precision, the rate of growth of money national income.

An increase in the understanding of the importance of time-lags in policy helped to do two further things. Monetary policy was seen as being ineffective in the short run but powerful in the long run. This fitted in well with the strengthening view that government policy should be aimed only at providing a stable framework within which the private sector could operate, not at close control of spending within the economy. In addition, the feeling that there were long time-lags in economic policy threw even more doubt on fiscal policy which had been largely used as an instrument to manipulate the economy in the short run.

Also crucial in the changing academic pattern was the increasing acceptance of the monetary history of the USA, written by the American economists Milton Friedman and Anna Schwartz. This appeared to show a close long-run relationship between the rate of growth of the money supply and changes in the price level. In other words, we had increasing empirical support for the version of the quantity theory which saw V and Y as constant and M being the principal determinant of the price level. In a time of great worry about the rate of inflation, this was very attractive.

What remained to be shown was that government **could** succeed in controlling the money supply. However, we have seen that two of the barriers to such control which had existed in the 1960s had been removed – the unwillingness of government to vary interest rates because of its dominating concern with financing budget deficits; and the existence of fixed exchange rates.

Research of the late 1970s and 1980s has produced much more ambiguous results regarding the nature of demand for money functions, and there has recently been strong criticism of the work of Friedman and Schwartz. In 1976, however, many economists found the work of monetarists very convincing and this added to the likelihood that monetarist policies would replace the enfeebled Keynesianism.

6.1.4 The part played by the IMF

Another result of the events of the early 1970s was the development of massive balance of payments deficits by the UK. A consequence of this was that the government needed to seek large loans from the International Monetary Fund. The Fund, unable to provide anything but a small proportion of the amounts needed by world governments in the aftermath of the oil price rise, was in the mood to seek stringent policy changes from the borrowing governments. It did so in the UK case and considerably influenced the decision of the Labour government to set regular money supply targets from 1976 on, and to attempt to reduce the public sector borrowing requirement (PSBR). This was but another influence on the eclipse of fiscal by monetary policy.

6.1.5 Ideology

By the mid-1970s, too, the welfare state philosophy which had seen poverty and unemployment as the responsibility of the whole economy was heavily under attack. We were witnessing the beginning of the return to 'Victorian values' with the stress placed on self-reliance and personal responsibility. Workers came to be seen as causing unemployment through the limitations they placed on the ways in which their labour could be used and through their demand for higher wages than the country could afford.

Going was the view that the cause of economic hardship was outside the control of individuals and that therefore governments, on behalf of the community, were required to do something about it. The vocabulary of 'equality' and 'redistribution' was being replaced by that of 'productivity' and 'incentives'. 'Job loss' became 'job saving'. The notion of the 'beneficent public sector' was being replaced by that of the 'muddling, bureaucratic public sector'. We were on our way from 'nationalisation' to 'privatisation'.

How this can be accounted for, other than simply as a reaction to what came before, is difficult to say. It is clear, though, that the considerable change in political ideas played a major role in the replacement of one set of economic policies by another, and in the rise of monetary policy.

6.2 THE MEDIUM-TERM FINANCIAL STRATEGY

The medium-term financial strategy (MTFS) was announced by

the Conservative government in the budget speech of 1980. Its stated aims were to bring down the rate of inflation and to bring about the conditions necessary for the growth of both output and employment. The first of these aims was thought to require control of the rate of growth of the money supply. Thus, the central element of the strategy was the announcement of target rates of growth of £M$_3$ for up to four years ahead.

We have seen that such target ranges had been a feature of economic policy from 1976. What was new about the medium-term financial strategy was the consistency with which it signalled a complete break from earlier Keynesian macroeconomic policy-making. This was especially true in the belief which it showed in the operation of the private market economy. Such an economy it was felt, would respond quickly to changes in economic circumstances through rapid changes in relative prices. It would also lead to higher and more stable levels of real income.

A consequence of this was the belief that countering inflation was the principal if not the only aim of macroeconomic policy since it was thought to pose a serious threat to the way in which markets work. To function properly, markets are held to require clear, unambiguous signals in the form of changing relative prices. Inflation can be seen to obscure such signals through causing confusion between absolute and relative price changes. In this way, theoretical support is provided for the public dislike of inflation.

The MTFS further accepted the quantity theory of money with which we have dealt at length in this book. Accepted also was the notion that the government could control successfully the money supply. Thus the decision of the government in 1979 to remove exchange controls and to allow the exchange rate to float more freely than it had done between 1972 and 1979 was a necessary prerequisite for the MTFS.

In addition, considerable stress was placed on expectations. Slowing down of money supply growth, it was argued, would cause money national income to grow more slowly than before. However, if workers did not believe that prices would increase less rapidly in the future, and so kept pushing wages up, then for quite a long time real income and employment would fall instead of the rate of price increase slowing down.

The government could not directly control the rate of growth of money wages in the private sector and could not, it was held, therefore be responsible for the resulting unemployment. What government could do, though, was to persuade people of the firmness of its intention to bring down prices, both by its statement and by succeeding in keeping the rate of growth of the money supply within its target range.

Then, the theory continued, workers would realise that they were causing unemployment. They would allow earnings to rise more slowly. Real wages would begin to fall, output and employment would rise and inflation would be curbed.

6.2.1 The government and economic growth

Success in the second aim of the MTFS also hinged on a belief in the working of private sector markets. Growth was held to depend on the willingness of workers to work hard and to acquire the skills needed by the economy, and the willingness of entrepreneurs to show initiative and to take risks. Again, government was not thought able to influence directly these supply side factors. All it could do was to provide incentives; or, rather, to reduce the extent to which government behaviour was responsible for disincentives in the economy. Principally, that meant acting to reduce the levels of taxation and to lower interest rates.

6.2.2 The implications for public expenditure

Since the government accepted the argument explained in Chapter 4 of links between the PSBR, the money supply and the level of interest rates, the MTFS had to aim at reducing the size of the PSBR. Since the government also wished to lower tax rates, it was clear that public expenditure would have to be reduced in real terms. Hence, the first statement of the strategy envisaged public expenditure falling from 42 per cent of gross domestic product (GDP) in 1979–80 to below 40 per cent of it by 1983–84.

Also implied was a change in the approach towards the public sector from a consideration of the quantity of resources it used to a concentration on the level, in cash terms, of its expenditure. A movement towards this new position had started in 1976 with the introduction of cash limits into public expenditure planning.

Success or failure in the management of the public sector will be judged then, using the values of the MTFS, solely in financial terms – a complete contrast with Keynesian public sector management. This had involved making medium-term estimates of the total resources available in the economy and subtracting the forecast resource use of the private sector. Public sector expenditure plans would then aim to use the remaining resources. The amount of money spent by the public sector became a secondary consideration. This system was known as 'volume planning'. Within the overall volume of resources thought to be available to the government, stress was placed on efficiency of resource use.

It is plain that this system rejected the notion that the public and private sectors were in competition for resources. Rather, public expenditure was thought to encourage private sector investment through providing direct markets for private sector goods and services and through the Keynesian multiplier process. The attitude in the MTFS, by contrast, is that increases in public expenditure are likely to be at the expense of private sector consumption and investment.

6.2.3 'Crowding-out'

This idea (sometimes known as 'resource crowding-out') is only part of the general 'crowding-out' debate concerning the relationship between the public and private sectors. Most of this difference in opinion has dealt with the possibility that increased public sector borrowing might lead to increased interest rates which, in turn, might discourage private sector investment and expenditure on durable consumer goods ('financial crowding-out').

The Keynesian approach, concentrating as it did on economies with considerable amounts of unemployment and hence unused resources, held that the public and private sectors could grow together. The school of thought in which the MTFS has its roots sees available resources as always being fully used. If this is so, the two sectors can be seen to be in competition for funds and for resources.

6.2.4 A summary of the MTFS

The principal points of the MTFS were:

(a) the setting of medium-term money supply growth targets;
(b) the aim to encourage the private sector by reducing interest rates and tax rates; and

(c) the intention to reduce the real level of public expenditure and the share of public expenditure in GDP.

6.2.5 The medium term: rules vs discretion

To understand fully the extent of the change which had taken place in economic policy, one needs to contrast the strategy outlined above with the view that had been widely accepted in the 1950s and 1960s. This was that the government should attempt to 'fine tune' the economy; that is, it should attempt to manipulate tax rates, interest rates and the level of government expenditure so as to achieve several policy aims, notably low unemployment, low rates of inflation and a satisfactory balance of payments.

This view required great faith in the ability of the government to forecast what was likely to happen to those economic variables outside its direct control (e.g. private sector investment, the value of exports and the prices of imported raw materials). Also, the government needed to be able to predict accurately the impact on the economy of changes in government policy – both the size of its impact and the time period over which it would occur.

Knowing how long it would take for economic policy changes to work was important if the government hoped to offset undesirable economic fluctuations which it could see coming. For example, suppose forecasters were saying that unemployment would reach high levels in, say, eighteen months' time unless the government altered its present policy. Then, it was vital to feel that something could be done to boost demand in perhaps three months' time, output in nine months' time and employment in possibly fifteen months' time.

Believing such things to be possible, governments felt that they could prevent the large fluctuations in economic activity and the very high levels of unemployment which had been experienced prior to the Second World War. This type of policy was known as **discretionary** policy, because policy instruments were changed at the discretion of the government in accordance with the view it held of what was likely to happen in the future.

The obvious difficulty was that if the forecasters were wrong, or if the government was wrong about the size or the timing of the impact of its policies, discretionary policy might make things worse, not better. Thus, arguments arose about the length of time-lags in government policy – that is, the length of time between recognizing the need for action and when the actions taken had the desired effect in the economy. More important than the length of time-lags was their variability. If, say, a change in tax rate took six months to work on some occasions but much shorter or longer periods on others, it would be extremely difficult, if not impossible, to control the economy with any degree of precision.

Monetarists did not accept that fiscal policy could be of much help at all in running the economy. Indeed, the common opinion among them was that manipulating government expenditure and taxation to try to reduce unemployment faced problems over time-lags **and** (as we have seen in our outline of the 'crowding-out' debate) was likely to interfere with incentives within the private sector. Many monetarists, on the other hand, did think that changes in the money supply could have powerful effects on both prices and, for some time, on real income. However, they also believed that monetary policy involved long and variable time-lags and so could not be used to 'fine tune' the economy – that is, governments should only, they felt, intervene in the private sector to ensure that markets operated freely.

A supporting argument for this view was that frequent government policy changes added to the uncertainty of investors and other decision-makers within the market. Governments were, however, held responsible for the rate of growth of the money supply and had to have some sort of monetary policy. The answer to the problem was thus seen in terms of the laying down of a monetary rule stating by how much the money supply would be allowed to grow over the subsequent four to five years. The market would then be left free to operate, secure in the knowledge that the rule would be upheld.

We have already seen several important implications of stating such a rule:

(a) the government must be able to keep to its rule;
(b) people in the economy must believe that the government intends to and is able to keep to its rule; and
(c) the government must be correct in its view of the medium-term relationships between the rate of growth of the money stock and unemployment.

To these we can add:

(d) in order to set sensible medium-term figures, the government must be able to make some accurate forecasts about what is likely to happen in the future, though the forecasts needed will be much more limited than those required for a Keynesian approach to the management of the economy.

6.2.6 A monetary rule example

An exercise in setting a monetary rule may then go something like this:

Aim: to bring down the rate of growth of the money stock steadily so that the rate of inflation is steadily reduced. **Assumptions**: present rate of growth of the money supply is 12 per cent; the rate of growth of productivity in the economy is 1.5 per cent; the size of the labour force is constant and therefore, with no change in unemployment, output would increase by 1.5 per cent per annum. If there were no inflation and if the velocity of money were constant, the money supply would need to grow by 1.5 per cent per annum to allow the extra output to be purchased.

Targets: the government might then say that it would bring down the rate of growth of the money stock towards an ultimate target of 1.5 per cent per annum. They may declare a target range for its growth of say 7 to 11 per cent in Year 1; 6 to 10 per cent in Year 2; 5 to 9 per cent in Year 3; and 4 to 8 per cent in Year 4. This may seem a rather slow descent towards the ultimate target, but these were the target ranges set out by the UK government in its **Financial Statement and Budget Report** in 1980.

Problems: achieving the target; convincing workers that inflation will fall. Suppose instead that workers believe inflation will rise to 15 per cent in Year 1 and they act so as to increase their money wages in that year by 16 per cent in order to increase the purchasing power of their wages by 1 per cent. Assume further that the outcome in Year 1 is a 15 per cent inflation rate and a 10 per cent rate of increase in the money supply. It is clear, then, that if the velocity of money is constant, less output will be able to be purchased than in the previous year. Stocks will build up; after a time, firms will reduce their output, and, some time later, unemployment will increase.

The outcome in Year 2 will depend on such things as whether the level of unemployment and/or government statements will cause workers to lower their wage demands; and whether the higher unemployment and/or changes in legislation affecting the bargaining power of trades unions will lessen the ability of workers to achieve their wage aims.

It follows that a medium-term strategy can have short-run effects. Consequently, it must be believed that any short-run costs of the strategy (for example, high unemployment) will be more than offset by the gains which will result when the strategy finally succeeds.

6.2.7 Problems in controlling public expenditure

The government faced three particular problems in attempting to reduce the real level of public expenditure. These were:

(a) It wished to increase expenditure on defence and on the maintenance of domestic law and order.

(b) There are large areas of expenditure (e.g. unemployment benefits) where the government determines only the rate to be paid but the total amount spent depends also on the number of people eligible for payment and on the proportion of those eligible who actually claim. These expenditures are 'demand-determined' and account for over 35 per cent of total public expenditure. In the recession which began in the second half of 1979, unemployment rose rapidly and the total amount of demand-determined expenditure had to rise. Worse still, when unemployment rises, taxation revenue falls.

(c) There was a significant amount of public expenditure which, in 1981, the central government did not control directly. Most important was local authority expenditure. The government attempted to force local authorities to reduce their spending by cutting Treasury contributions to them through the rate-support grant. This helped to lower the PSBR. However, local authorities responded by pushing up local rates. That meant that the PSBR was being reduced not by cutting expenditure but by raising taxation. The government also found that additional losses of public corporations during the recession had to be financed.

Difficulties of this kind made the MTFS especially difficult to implement during a recession.

6.2.8 PSBR: projections and out-turns

Precise targets for the PSBR have not been part of the MTFS. This is principally because of the great difficulty in forecasting it. Instead, the government has contented itself with projections of PSBR based upon an assumed rate of growth of GDP and on public expenditure plans thought to be 'broadly compatible' with the monetary objectives.

The 1980 **Financial Statement and Budget Report**, provided the figures given in Table 6.1. In the event, public expenditure proved much more difficult to control than the government had anticipated and, as a percentage of GDP, rose significantly from 40.5 per cent in 1978–79 to a peak of 44 per cent in 1981–82, declining only very slightly to 43.5 per cent in 1982–83. A result of this was that, despite the fact that the overall burden of taxation did not fall and despite the fact that the PSBR was kept lower than it would otherwise have been through the sale of public sector assets, government plans for the PSBR were not fulfilled. This can be seen by comparing Tables 6.1 and 6.2.

Table 6.1   PSBR as percentage of GDP at market prices(planned)

1980–81	3.75
1981–82	3
1982–83	2.25
1983–84	1.5

Table 6.2   PSBR as percentage of GDP at market prices(actual)

1980–81	5.7
1981–82	3.5
1982–83	3.25
1983–84	3.25*

prices(planned)
* Estimated figure
Source: Economic Progress Reports

6.3 THE DIFFICULTIES OF RECENT YEARS

In Section 6.2 we said that the central feature of the MTFS was a rule governing the growth of the money stock. It is central in two senses. Firstly, since one purpose of the strategy is to ensure consistency among a number of financial magnitudes, the desired rate of monetary growth is, in this sense, determining the size of the other components of the strategy.

Secondly, it is hoped that projecting the growth of the money stock into the medium-term future will have a beneficial effect on people's behaviour by giving them confidence in the future course of the economy. We have stressed that, for this to work, the government must be seen to be both willing and able repeatedly to achieve its publicly announced targets. In this instance at least, to fail may be worse than never to have tried.

Table 6.3 shows the authorities' announced target rates of growth and the actual out-turns of the various monetary aggregates.

From the table, a number of features stand out. Firstly, taking $£M_3$ as the longest running target, the out-turn has been within the target range only four times in ten attempts. Secondly, this is in spite of the authorities having chosen quite wide target ranges. In years when the range was 8 to 12 per cent, for example, with

Table 6.3 Growth of monetary aggregates: targets and outturns

Date	Period of target	Aggregate	Target growth % p.a.	Actual growth % p.a.
Dec. 1976	Year to April 1977	$£M_3$	9–13	7.7
Mar. 1977	Year to April 1978	$£M_3$	9–13	16.0
April 1978	Year to April 1979	$£M_3$	8–12	10.9
Nov. 1978	Year to Oct. 1979	$£M_3$	8–12	13.3
June 1979	June 1979 to April 1980	$£M_3$	7–11	10.3
Nov. 1979	June 1979 to Oct. 1980	$£M_3$	7–11	17.8
Mar. 1980	Feb. 1980 to April 1981	$£M_3$	7–11	18.5
Mar. 1981	Feb. 1981 to April 1982	$£M_3$	6–10	14.5
Mar. 1982	Feb. 1982 to April 1983	$£M_3$	8–12	11.1
		M_1	8–12	14.3
		PSL_2	8–12	11.3
Mar. 1983	Feb. 1983 to April 1984	$£M_3$	7–11	9.8*
		M_1	7–11	11.0*
		PSL_2	7–11	12.3*
Mar. 1984	Feb. 1984 to April 1985	$£M_3$	6–10	
		M_0	4–8	

* Estimates

Sources: *BEQB* and *Financial Statistics*, HMSO, various issues.

a mid-point of 10, the margin of permitted deviation was plus or minus 20 per cent.

Thirdly, the 'misses' have nearly all been in the direction of overshoot, sometimes by very large margins. Between 1979 and 1981, for example, actual growth was approximately twice the mid-point of the target range.

Fourthly, and partly as a result of the unhappy results for 1979–81, the authorities actually raised the target range above the 1979–81 level, in spite of professed commitments to 'stricter' monetary control. Plainly, all has not gone well and some explanation is necessary. What such an explanation reveals is just how varied a range of influences – the level of demand in the world economy, the level of overseas interest rates, government spending, people's expectations about inflation – bears upon the actual outcome and makes monetary control so difficult.

We mentioned in Section 4.5 the possibility that the demand for bank lending is neither stable nor interest-sensitive. Certainly it seems likely that the authorities underestimated the private sector's demand for bank credit in 1979 and 1980. Factors promoting the strong demand included the switch from direct to indirect taxation, giving a sharp boost to inflation and, in 1980 in particular, an unexpectedly sharp downturn in world trade forcing firms into 'distress borrowing' at the same time as minimum lending rate at 17 per cent encouraged short-term bank borrowing in preference to long-term bond issues. The authorities also were faced with an unexpectedly large PSBR which necessitated some borrowing from the monetary sector.

In 1981–82 public sector finances were again a source of monetary expansion, though the origin of the problem lay elsewhere. For several months in 1981 a strike by civil servants delayed the collection of tax revenue. To cover what was always hoped to be a short-term problem, the issue of extra gilt-edged stock would not have been appropriate (even if it had been practically possible at such short notice) and the Bank was consequently forced into larger than anticipated bill sales to the monetary sector in the manner and with the consequences described at the end of Section 3.4.

Changes in banks' marketing strategy may also have had some relevance to the rapid growth in 1981–82. In the early part of this period banks entered the housing mortgage field, competing strongly with building societies for a share of this market. It is hard to know just how much of bank mortgage lending was a substitute for building society lending and how much was a genuine addition. Since all bank lending, the creation of bank deposits, adds to the money stock, however, there can be no doubt about this effect. But, to the extent that some of it represented a reduction in building society lending, there may have been some small offsetting fall in velocity.

One further incident, which was almost certainly cosmetic in the sense that its addition to monetary growth was compensated by a reduction in non-bank lending and, therefore, had little relevance to actual expenditure, was the removal of the 'corset' in June 1980. We described in Section 4.2 the way in which this direct limitation on the growth of bank deposits encouraged firms to obtain credit by the issue of commercial bills 'accepted' by banks. If contemporary estimates of this 'bill-leak' at £3 bn. were correct, and if, on termination of the supplementary special deposits scheme, the whole of the £3 bn. was substituted by bank borrowing, then this may have accounted for four of the percentage points in the very high growth figure for $£M_3$ of 18.5 per cent in 1980–81.

Lastly, we have to consider the use of short-term interest rates for monetary control purposes in the light of other government policy objectives. We may assume that a rise in interest rates, intended to restrict monetary growth, will always be unwelcome from most other points of view. It means capital losses for those holding short-term financial assets and, if movements in short-term rates become interpreted as a pointer to long-term rates, then the latter may also rise, causing capital losses on longer dated assets, raising mortgage rates and reducing investment expenditure.

In recent years, however, a more pressing concern than any of these has been the effect upon the exchange rate. A rise in short-term interest rates clearly makes those assets yielding these rates more attractive then they previously were to both domestic and overseas purchasers. Overseas buyers pay either in their own currency, which is subsequently exchanged for sterling, or in sterling which they have themselves acquired. In either event, there is a rise in the exchange rate. In certain circumstances this may assist in the pursuit of other policy objectives. By making imports cheaper, for example, it helps reduce domestic inflation. By the same token, however, it raises the export price of UK goods and depresses the demand for them. That means that it worsens the balance of payments on current account by making export industries less competitive internationally.

One dramatic accompaniment to the government's monetary and fiscal policies since 1979 has been the rise in unemployment. However much some economists may have regarded it as predictable, it was unintended and certainly unwelcome. Part of the explanation was the unexpectedly severe world recession referred to earlier. In these circumstances where demand for UK exports was falling and unemployment rising, there was a lot to be said against making things worse by **raising** interest rates thus pushing the exchange rate up.

One obvious way of explaining the overshoot of 1981–82, given a system of interest rate control, is to argue that interest rates were not raised sufficiently to reduce the demand for bank credit. In the same period, the effective exchange rate fell by 10 per cent, giving some much needed assistance to UK exporters. With higher interest rates, it is reasonable to infer that this depreciation would not have happened and unemployment would have risen even more rapidly than it did. We know that a Labour government sacrificed a monetary growth target in 1977–78 because the required level of interest rates would have conflicted with its exchange rate policy; and 1981–82 may have been another example.

6.4 THE FAILURE OF THE NEW MONETARY POLICY

In the previous section, we have considered two areas of failure of the new monetary policy – the failure to achieve announced money supply targets, and the need to keep interest rates high with undesirable side-effects in the attempt to achieve them. In one sense it might be argued that the failure to achieve money supply targets means that the policy has not yet adequately been tried. This is a poor defence, however, since the belief that the money supply is controllable by the government is an essential part of the support for the policy. Impractical policies should be confined to textbooks.

An alternative way of judging success is to consider the overall aims of the policy. These were, remember, the reduction of the rate of inflation and the bringing about of the conditions necessary for growth and increased employment. Certainly the rate of

Table 6.4 Growth of the money supply and inflation

Year	Rate of growth $£M_3$ p.a.	Rate of inflation % p.a.
1979–80	13.7	13.4
1980–81	11.8	18.0
1981–82	12.5	11.9
1982–83	11.1	8.6
1983–84	9.8	4.7

* Estimated figure

Source: *Economic Trends,* HMSO, Jan. 1984, Tables 52 and 42.

inflation has fallen, coming down from 18 per cent in 1980–81 to 4.7 per cent in 1983–84 (see Table 6.4). It is not obvious, however, that this decline can be best explained (or even explained at all) by the theory underlying the new policy.

One problem is that there has been little apparent correlation between the rate of growth of the money supply and the rate of inflation. This issue is complicated by the existence of various arguments about the length of time-lags expected in monetary policy. We have seen that monetarists used to think that there were long and variable time-lags in monetary policy and argued that a close relationship between the rate of growth of the money supply and the rate of inflation would only be observed in the long run. Recently, monetarists stressing the desirability of assuming rational expectations in the economy (see Section 5.3.7) have provided theoretical arguments against such time-lags. Other monetarists have argued that whereas long time-lags once existed, there has been a dramatic shortening of them. Such arguments, however, are unsupported and sometimes seem to be rather desperate attempts to make the facts fit the theory.

Another complication concerns the central role initially given to reduction of the PSBR so as to keep down interest rates while achieving money supply targets. We have shown (in the appendix to Ch. 4) that the theoretical relationship among these variables has not existed in practice. Further, even if we had been able to discern a close actual relationship between the PSBR and the rate of growth of the money supply, we could have interpreted this in a straightforward Keynesian fashion. The government, we might have said, has been using a deflationary **fiscal** policy, causing aggregate demand and income to be lower than they would otherwise have been. We would have expected a reduction for this reason in the demand for bank loans and, hence, in the money supply.

Coming to conclusions regarding the second aim of the strategy is fraught with difficulty. One of the problems in judging any avowedly 'medium-term' policy is that the 'medium term' can be very elastic. The economy seems to be forever 'on the right lines', moving towards 'light at the end of the tunnel' and 'steering a fair course'. It is always possible for those who promise results only at the end of the medium term, when asked how long such a term may be, to reply in effect that 'the medium term is as long as it takes for the results of a medium-term strategy to appear'.

As we write (March 1984), output is growing steadily but slowly. Unemployment is no longer increasing but there are few brave enough to forecast that it will fall significantly in the near future. The rate of growth of output is particularly modest given the depth of the recession from which the economy has been 'recovering' now for nearly three years, yet there are doubts whether even this modest growth rate will be sustained. British industry may or may not be in a more competitive position internationally than in 1979. If it is, it is by no means clear that the gains in relative productivity will be permanent. The returns on the real side of the economy are meagre indeed.

Against them, one must place continuing economic and social costs of high unemployment. Future gains, if and when they come, must be heavily discounted to allow for years of loss. Also, it must be borne in mind that those who eventually gain will not be the same people as those who have lost through the restrictive policies of recent years. The unequal way in which the burden of unemployment is spread throughout the population makes it much more difficult to compare the costs of the new policy with the gains which it still claims it will produce.

QUESTIONS

Essay questions

1. Summarise and evaluate monetarist recommendations for macroeconomic policy. (O)

2. Discuss the view that a government can moderate the rate of inflation by exercising an appropriate restraint on the rate of increase of the supply of money. (WJEC)

3. Contrast the neo-Keynesian theory with that of the monetarist school as propounded by Friedman. What practical problems arise in the implementation of monetary policy? (ICMA)

4. To bring down the rate of inflation 'it is necessary to reduce the rate of growth of the money supply and therefore of government expenditure'. Discuss. (O)

Discussion questions

1. What are the difficulties involved in deciding whether a particular government policy has succeeded or failed?

2. Apply the results of this discussion to a consideration of the MTFS. Has anything changed in the British economy since this book was written (March 1984) which might affect one's judgement as to the success or failure of the MTFS?

3. Consider which groups of people gain and which lose from the operation of the MTFS. Does the fact that the distribution of income is altered by macroeconomic policy make it harder to judge its performance?

4. Consider all the meanings that you can find in economics for 'short term', 'medium term' and 'long term'. What meaning can you give them from a policy point of view? What is the relevance of Keynes's famous statement that 'in the long run we are all dead'?

BIBLIOGRAPHY

Artis M J, Lewis M K 1981 **Monetary control in the United Kingdom**.
   Philip Allan
Backhouse R 1983 **Macroeconomics and the British economy**. Martin
   Robertson
Bain A D 1982 **The control of the money supply**. Penguin
Brown A J 1983 'Friedman and Schwartz on the United Kingdom' in **Monet-
   ary trends in the United Kingdom**. Bank of England Panel of Academic
   Consultants Panel Paper No. 22
Brown R 1981 **Monetary control in Britain 1971–1981**. Banking Information
   Service
Brown R 1982 **A guide to monetary policy**. Banking Information Service
Carter H, Partington I 1981 **Applied economics in banking and finance**.
   Oxford University Press
Challen D, Hagger A J, Hardwick P 1984 **Unemployment and inflation in
   the UK**. Longman
Crockett A 1979 **Money. Theory, policy and institutions** 2nd edn. Nelson
Cross R 1982 **Economic theory and policy in the UK**. Martin Robertson
Dennis G E J 1981 **Monetary economics**. Longman
Desai M 1981 **Testing monetarism**. Francis Pinter
Dow S, Earl P 1982 **Money matters. A Keynesian approach to monetary
   economics**. Martin Robertson
Gowland D H 1982 **Controlling the money supply**. Croom Helm
Gowland D H 1983 **Modern economic analysis** vol. 2 Butterworth
Greenaway D, Shaw G K 1983 **Macroeconomics: theory and policy in the
   UK**. Martin Robertson
Havrilesky T M, Boorman J T (eds) 1980 **Current issues in monetary
   theory and policy** 2nd edn. AHM Publishing Corporation
Hendry D F, Ericsson N R 1983 'An econometric appraisal of Friedman
   and Schwartz' "Monetary trends in . . . the United Kingdom"' in
   Monetary trends in the United Kingdom. Bank of England Panel of
   Academic Consultants Panel Paper No. 22
Hockley G C 1970 **Monetary policy and public finance**. Routledge and
   Kegan Paul

BIBLIOGRAPHY

Johnston R B 1984 **Demand for non-interest-bearing money in the UK.** HM Treasury

Laidler D 1977 **The demand for money: Theories and evidence** 3rd edn. Intertext Books

Lipsey R G 1983 **An introduction to positive economics** 6th edn. Weidenfeld and Nicolson.

Llewellyn D, Dennis G E J, Hall J B, Nellis J G 1982 **The framework of UK monetary policy** Heinemann Educational Books

Maunder P (ed.) 1980 **The British economy in the 1970s.** Heinemann Educational Books

Morgan B 1978 **Monetarists and Keynesians – their contribution to monetary theory.** Macmillan

Morris D (ed.) 1979 **The economic system in the UK** 2nd edn. Oxford University Press

Parkin M, Bade R 1982 **Modern macroeconomics.** Philip Allan

Pierce D G, Shaw D M 1974 **Monetary economics.** Butterworth

Prest A R, Coppock D J (eds) 1982 **The UK economy** 9th edn. Weidenfeld and Nicolson

Rowan D C 1983 **Output, inflation and growth** 3rd edn. Macmillan

Shaw G K 1977 **An introduction to the theory of macroeconomic policy** 3rd edn. Martin Robertson

Shone R 1984 **Issues in macroeconomics.** Martin Robertson

Surrey M J C (ed.) 1976 **Macroeconomic themes.** Oxford University Press

Vane H, Thompson J 1979 **Mor.etarism: theory, evidence and policy.** Martin Robertson

Vane H, Thompson J 1982 **An introduction to macroeconomic policy.** Wheatsheaf

Westaway A J, Weyman-Jones T G 1977 **Macroeconomics: theory, evidence and policy.** Longman

Wilson K 1982 **British Financial Institutions.** Pitman

INDEX

153

INDEX